# Diary of a Wimpy Eventer

## Part Three

How to get yourself off

"You always look so happy when you're riding…."

www.wimpyeventer.com


Printed in Great Britain.

Written, designed and produced by Gary and Victoria Brant
(Daddy Carrot and the Wimpy Eventer)

Beautifully illustrated by Bonny Snowdon Fine Art



Edition 1
ISBN: 978-1-5272-3404-8

**With thanks to…**

My horses.

Every single one that has graced my life and that has touched my heart. Without them, none of this would exist. Without them, I would be a very different human (probably a wealthier one).

We owe so much to our horses; the tears that fall into their manes, the squeals with joy we share galloping down a stubble field, yet they remain so unassuming.

Horses do not know that we've had a bad day, yet they are always there.

For all of them.

So, here's the deal… my first ever event season ended on an absolute high. My placing at Norton Disney was the absolute icing on the 2017 cake. I came from the depths of confidence hell to conquer a BE100, complete several events and be a whisker away from Badminton Grassroots.

I had two amazing horses, ending the season buying my darling Bender (Sir Bentley) who came from a racehorse rehoming charity and he fast became the apple of my eye alongside Pat. I was certain he would be destined for Horse of The Year show, as Pat was for Badminton, and I felt full to the brim with love and excitement.

But as with anything involving horses, basking in momentary bliss is exactly that. Momentary. You soon wake up to a cold, dark December and wonder what the hell you were thinking taking up this hobby. Instead you could have been cross stitching patterns of Salisbury Cathedral onto a piece of cloth in the warm, dry comfort of your front room. There would be no hay to buy, no mountains of sh*t to pick up in the field, no mud to scrape off before getting freezing cold and wet out on a very average ride. But there is something that keeps us going, there is something I struggle to put into words that keeps me from buying several thread colours and a donut bum cushion. It is that musky horse smell, the feeling of exhaustion, but still the remarkable ability to take on the world of full wheelbarrow pushing through a hail storm. It's the days you sob so hard into your horses' neck because only HE can understand. That is why we are all here, why you have picked up this book. You and me. We are those people and you get it, just like I do.

I hope you learn as much from this journey as I have, and I hope you can now see that if everything went according to plan, I'd have won the lottery years ago and they'd be no need for this nonsense at all!

## January 2018

## MOMENTARY Bliss

Now, with the event season over what I should probably have done is turn my horse away for a little rest. This appears to be common practice in the eventing world and I do get it, but Pat is a total knob after time off (and during for that matter). So instead I thought I'd tackle some good positive dressage outings, while we were in the right frame of mind, and leave his holidays until the New Year.

**January 5th 2018**

Tonight we ventured back to my favourite venue; Hill House Equestrian, for the second instalment of the winter dressage league!!

Yesterday I practiced my medium trot down a field out hacking and taught him to 'go go go' on the aid, not 'go in a minute' a year after I ask! You don't have long in a 20x40 to show off medium strides, so I want to get better at it! And of course, the best time to do that is the day before the show on the grass verge!

I had a very sluggish attempt at Novice 27 where he got away with bobbling round and me working very hard to keep him forward!! We got 72.16% and second place. I then got my act together and kicked him up the arse a bit for E50 to achieve our best Elementary result I've had to date!! 69.46% and the WIN!!! Simple changes actually happened tonight too!! Now, without getting too big for my boots, I have worked really hard over the last 7 years on his flatwork (mostly due to a fear of leaving the ground) and it really showed in these tests. I know him inside out and I know how much I can push before he boils over into a snorting, tail swishing twonk!

You can only accumulate league points at the highest level, so that's two wins in a row for us! I feel so happy, so happy to be improving, and happy to keep working at it too... maybe Bender will get a turn soon?

With Bender going SO well and after a little quiet time and time to settle in, I had really begun to up his work load and retraining. He had such an AMAZING attitude to life, that even after a week off I could tack him up and he was just like an old man with his slippers on and getting him going had me sweating. He would stand like a rock for me to get on and wouldn't ever dream of moving unless he has to.  From the outset I decided to treat him like the old arm chair ride that I wanted him to become, and he really was 80% there already - some race horse eh?!

I hadn't really asked too much of him in the contact yet either, mainly because we had been concentrating on leg aids (forwards) and my seat aids for stopping! But we did have stop and go installed and so it was time to learn the frames that are required for his muscular comfort.

I am a very firm believer in 'building the bridge' - developing the muscles over the spine that my fat arse bounces on (especially with a TB having been inverted for most of their ridden lives), how can you get the head and neck lower if the bridge has collapsed under you...? A strong bridge is vital for them to drop the head and neck comfortably and be able to work in 'the outline' we ask… Or that's the way the theory of biomechanics works in my head!

Up until this point the contact and head/neck position had been a mixture of giraffe (for his balance) and peacock (because it avoids dealing with the contact). In a nutshell, I would keep a low, wide but consistent contact and do a lot of kicking!

To help him understand a bit more, I would make the giraffe moments not so pleasant for him and give a firmer feel for him to know it's not ideal. And then lifting and vibrating the rein on the peacock moments to 'oi oi' him out of that dipping. Consequently, I would have a lovely soft contact after about 15 minutes and he was a very quick to learn when I spelt it out clearly. Of course, there would be inconsistencies but as soon as we had done a whole 20m circle with that shape and softness, he got to have a rest.

This is how I have trained all of my horses and it has worked for me. I'm no expert but clear, definitive instructions and very obvious rewards are always a good starting point in my book.

I then spend his second 15 minutes (I would only do half an hour with him at this stage) encouraging a longer, lower frame. So that would mean more kicking to get his belly up and feeding the rein out with little squeezes of pressure and release, giving away as much as he will take. By the 5 minute point the penny usually drops and he just exhales and plops into a lovely long frame. I always like to do this training in trot because you have that natural swing to work with. He would work like this consistently and very happily for 5 minutes through bends and changes of rein and gets lots of mega pats.

I just love this big boy so much. He's so loving and has firmly got his feet under the table.

Bender would do 3 days a week of work like this and 2-3 days on the long reins out around the little lanes near our yard. He wasn't massively settled for me to hack unescorted yet and this was something that started eating away at me a lot over the next couple of weeks.

**2nd November 2017**

Right... I'm on here because I need to offload. I don't often feel like this but today I do.

Do you ever just get days where you just want to cry.

I can't pin point a reason in particular either, I've asked the question; 'what's making you sad?' and I have no idea what the answer is.

People can look in from the outside and judge me wrongly sometimes, I hate that. I'm not rich in anything other than love, nor am I spoilt. Far from it. I work so hard that sometimes when you get criticized, it really feels very personal. Now, even though I work for myself, I still work a full time job - Crikey probably more hours than before! I still have a book to tie up in a fortnight and I have so much going on I just can't handle it.

I have a list as long as my arm to get done, 2 horses to ride (or Bender at the very least) and a mountain of washing to do. I need to go food shopping too because I have nothing to cook my Carrot for his tea, and actually all I want to do is curl up under a blanket and cry.

Yesterday I went out in my lunch break and followed the hunt on opening meet for a bit. Someone, a lovely, kind man who I have known for many, many years had a really nasty fall and was air lifted to hospital. Things aren't looking good at the moment. This has made me worry a lot for him and his lovely family too. My mind is all over the place.

I want to be a cheery ray of sunshine but today I feel like an oozing sack of rabbit droppings. I need a cuddle and a kick up the arse I think. It’s not often I have days like this but I feel so self-pitying and I bloody HATE it!

SNAP. OUT. OF. IT.!!

Seriously, I read this back now and I just want to slap myself! People have crappy days, people are allowed to wallow in their sads a bit, but please just think of how lucky you are, just for a second. Think about your current situation. Are you homeless? Are you in poverty to the point where you cannot eat unless you steal? Do you have the ability to breathe in and out and move around and feel something other than emptiness? How dare I not see that, and that’s the thing… On days like this, I need to realise, not just how pathetic it is complaining about trivial sh*t, but how lucky I actually am.

I have friends, a job, my horses, my husband, my health, a family… it's endless and yet I allow myself to complain like this. **Well LESSON NUMBER ONE**: Realise how lucky you are. Yes, things might not always feel perfect or go how you'd like them to. But you are so lucky to be alive. And for anyone feeling the same, go do what I just did... put on some mascara and go look in the mirror, tell yourself how wonderfully brilliant you are and flash yourself a boob... you'll laugh and then you'll realise things aren't so bad, just focus on that for five minutes whenever you feel those sads creeping in.

~

And when you do wake up not feeling your best, this is for you…

Imagine if today was all you had left to prove your worth, today is all you have left to make it count, to tell people how you feel and how much they mean to you. Imagine if today is your last ride, the last time you will ever get to feel the wind on your face and the cold in your toes as your horse gallops you across the grass.

What if it really was? How differently would today pan out for you?

Grab life by the big hairy testi-baubles today, don't wait for tomorrow because what if it doesn't come?

Love like it's now or never, ride like it's your last time and laugh like no one's watching you! You can be as wonderful as you like, you've got it in there… let it out. You won't regret it. Stop worrying about what you look like, how you come across and how life may or may not work out for you.

Live for today and I promise you, it will be the best bloody day you've ever had!

Go… bloody well do it now!!

Go on!!!

~

Anyhow... I digress! Back to my blissful November!

Now, two weeks in and I was happily hacking the boys out on ride and lead hacks and I was also climbing up the field gate to clamber onto my arm chair of a horse ... BENDER! He was SO relaxed out hacking with Pat, and as Daddy carrot is determined to ride more, I thought I had better prepare the horse for a novice jockey!

With Carrot wanting to set sail on his maiden Bender voyage that coming Sunday, I did everything I thought Daddy Carrot might do...I clambered onto him kicking him on the rump as I swung my leg over, took an age to do the girth up... fed him a whole packet of mints and guess what…? He did not move an inch!

Off we went striding out in front the whole way, hardly a spook or shy, and he is just the comfiest ride. We had a good trot and a little bit of canter (all in a pretty decent outline too) I was absolutely ecstatic with him! Like he had just got me round Badminton happy! It's the little things with horses that keep me going and this might have seemed such a small feat to most people but to me, it was the best day EVER!

**Minding your Manners**

When Bender arrived I think it is fair to say that he had been a bit of a Feral Beryl and just turned away in a field for a few years. I stand by the importance of good ground manners in all aspects of horsemanship, and sometimes these pony ground manners need keeping in check. It's also a great exercise to do when you don't feel like riding. It's good to see them working on the ground so you know areas you need to work on and see how they're improving.

Pat is VERY polite almost a little too shy to handle at times, so it just involves a lunge for him, lunging over a single pole on a big loop. Lots of forward and collecting in the trot, timing the pole on the ask for forward. It gets him pushing and round and working his muscles.

Bender next, back on the long reins... he has been getting a bit upset and excitable coming home from a walk/ride and it isn't very nice when you're on top, so today we went up and down the drive in both directions 5 or 6 times before I took him in a field away from everybody and did a ten minute lunge.

He settled down to work after 5 minutes of stressing, but as soon as he settled and did a few loops in a nice walk and trot, I put him away. He will do this every day now until we break his anxiety patterns. As soon as he is calm and does a little bit, back to the field as a reward.

There might be other ways of dealing with this, but I can't just ride him in the field next to his mates forever!! I'm toying with the idea of taking him on holiday down the road for a few weeks where they have arenas and coloured poles to break the attachment to home, but I'll do another week of today's routine and see where we are first.

Winter is hard to maintain momentum at the best of times, but it'll be so worth it in the end.

~

I was certainly finding this new horse and his stressy personality a challenge and the thought of taking him on a hack filled me with the fear of death. I was really struggling to bond with him because of that. We had a lot of issues with him in field too. Our yard is really small, just my two boys and Auntie Smurph with her two. It does mean that none of them would ever be alone in the field, but Bender wasn't happy unless Pat was there. This also meant my rides on Pat were being increasingly fraught too. Every time

I took Pat away, Bender would run the fence line until he was white with sweat and be constantly calling to his buddy. I tried separating the field in half, I tried a calmer, I tried having him next to the sheep and next to other horses, but he wasn't interested. He just pined for Pat.

My heart was breaking and I was very aware that all of the confidence that I had spent all season building was coming crashing down around my ears. Something had to change. I made a few calls to people that I thought might be able to take him on training livery but the costs were so high, I didn't really have the money to put him on full livery. So after a call with my friend Piers who owns a local equestrian centre, I packed Bender's suitcase and he got collected the next day. He was going on part livery at Willow Banks, where I could go and ride him myself to bring the costs down but where they would help me out with one end of the day.

I found myself struggling to muster the enthusiasm to go over there, my heart and my confidence were bruised, and although I loved the updates from Piers on how well he was going, I felt really sad about the whole situation and in honesty, full of regret.

**25th November 2017**

Here it is; honesty.

I haven't ridden for two weeks. 13 days to be precise, and I feel like total and utter sh*te about it.

There is a lot going on, it's too windy, the book, bla bla bla... EXCUSES!! My Mum has been in hospital since Wednesday and I've spent at least 4 hours a day with her the last two days, but again another excuse!

I'll tell you what, I feel selfish. I have two lovely horses - a luxury not everyone has but here I am, an ungrateful cow, not riding them.

I'm having a day of refocus. The book has gone to print today, the calendars are done and I have all Pink Thursday orders placed at the embroidery company.

I just feel all over the place, I want to relax and get excited about Christmas but I'm feeling constantly on edge about something.

It's not even 8.30 and I'm stressing, worrying and trying to be better. What I'm actually going to do is get dressed and go take Pat for a ride. Just us, just like it used to be.

These problems, worries and things I'm stressing about are so trivial. I know this, writing it all down helps me to see it. I haven't laughed in ages, so that's my aim today (look out). My hair is bushy, I have a spot, my eyebrows haven't been pencilled in and I've got eye bogeys, but HERE I AM. I've also got Ringworm, a wart on my foot and bunions (I'm dealing with it, alright!!).

If you are like me and have things on your plate that seem overwhelming, spew them out... I'm all ears. It's made me feel better already.

~

I did in fact go for a ride that day and I got a glimpse of what life used to be like when I wasn't stressing about Bender or money or something else! Why do we do this to ourselves? Put ourselves under this extreme pressure and get wound up about it? I was on a roll it seemed and the weekend had arrived, with no plans in place I had the bright idea of getting some photos together for the blog;

**27th November 2017**

Yesterday I managed to find a small slice of MOJO hidden in the depths of my moth ball infested spirit. I grabbed my Carrot and we headed off down to the yard.

I tacked up Pat and hopped on. I try not to plan what I'm going to do with him at the moment and just let the mood take us so I don't feel disheartened not having fulfilled the plan.

After 10 minutes of trotting about the field, I jumped my one and only jump (yes, we have more coming soon I hope) it was a 2ft ish cross pole and he felt GREAT and I felt SAFE. I had my new jumping saddle on, not the dressage saddle, so I thought 'bugger it, in for a penny'. I laid out a couple of placing poles and popped the cross to an upright. Now, anyone that knows me will know that I have a certain stigma with jumping uprights, I fear them falling more than any other jump. But without any more wings, I was forced into it.

We started it at about 85cms and jumped it in both directions, then popped it up to 105 and came around and jumped it a few more times without terrifying myself!!

I felt so happy to be doing a jump, it might sound pathetic, but I felt capable and confident and it really showed. The difference in my lower leg from just a couple of months ago is VERY noticeable and I definitely have the saddle to thank for that.

I also went over to see Bender that weekend too, he was going SO well and really wasn't that stressed at all over at Willow Banks, not like he was a home. He was often left until last in the stable without a fuss, and his educational work was coming on really well too. I was getting regular updates from Piers about his progress and videos of his ridden work which looked great, sympathetic but no nonsense. I had so much hope that we could work this out and get him home in a few weeks, it was back to momentary bliss….

## December 2017

## Times of Uncertainty

With a fairly noneventful week been and gone, my Mum given the all clear to come home in the next few days, I realised my anxiety was sky high again. I had been seriously nervous about something for a while. I couldn't put my finger on it, but I was about to find out. On Saturday 2nd December I had agreed to speak in public.

Most of you will by now, see through the façade of laughter and frivolity and know that I am a very insecure person underneath all the bravado. I've probably always been that way, and actually, I am usually quite comfortable in my own skin. But the thought of talking in front of people and on my own was one of the scariest things I could think of doing. But it was for the most wonderful charity and I couldn't possibly let them down with an excuse of FEAR… I was supposed to be the one conquering bloody fear, not running from it!

Anyway, we packed up the car with an over-night bag and made our way to the Wobbleberries Awards Night somewhere in the depths of the Midlands. I didn't prepare a speech or anything else for that matter, I wanted to be real and that doesn't come from reading off a sheet, or so I thought. So, with a rough introduction planned, I hoped other things would spring into my mind after that bit was over!

On arrival, I was greeted by the lovely founders of the Wobbleberries charity, and then by the other speaker for the evening, Andrew Hoy. Yeah that's right! The gold medallist, the international superhero. And media trained, comfortable speaking in public, Andrew was my partner in entertaining crime for the evening!

Anyway, I was up first so I was very relieved! I started by asking everyone in the room to shut their eyes… like always. I have found after doing a couple of these that people usually do as they're told when you've got a microphone in your hand and have the power to single them out at any moment! I then ask anyone who has felt fear around horses and riding, to raise their hand. Seriously, I feel something so magical when I'm standing in front of a room full of people all with their hands in the air. Even Andrew Hoy had his hand up. Covered head to toe in goose bumps, I welled up good and proper. Right there, in that moment… that was it, where I knew I felt at home; making a difference to these people. I talked about my experience with fear and I felt very emotional at one point, I dare say those there felt it too. I read a chapter from the book and that always gets me right in the feels. It's real you see, and although these books and social media, and all the cr*p that goes with it might look like a load of fun and be entertaining for everyone. My fear and journey is so real it physically hurts inside sometimes. I still battle with confidence and fear every single day, and I probably will for the whole of my life, but I won't ever let it beat me.

I have felt scared, I have felt desperation, I have felt like giving up on life, but I tell you what the most wonderful bit is, I have also found something from somewhere each time and fought through it all. You don't need to be the best, the bravest or create a Freddie Mercury legacy, you just need to find that strength to drag your arse out of the dark days. The rest you can worry about later. **LESSON NUMBER TWO: SURVIVAL.**

Survive, and worry about all the other sh*t later. Get through today, get through that week, get through that hour if that's as far as you can see. Just get through. Happiness, fulfilment, pride, comfort; that will all come in time, I promise. But you need to survive first. Chances are, as soon as you strip it down that far, you'll find yourself recovering much quicker and laughing at how a chocolate Santa, under the foil, looks awfully like a giant erect willy!

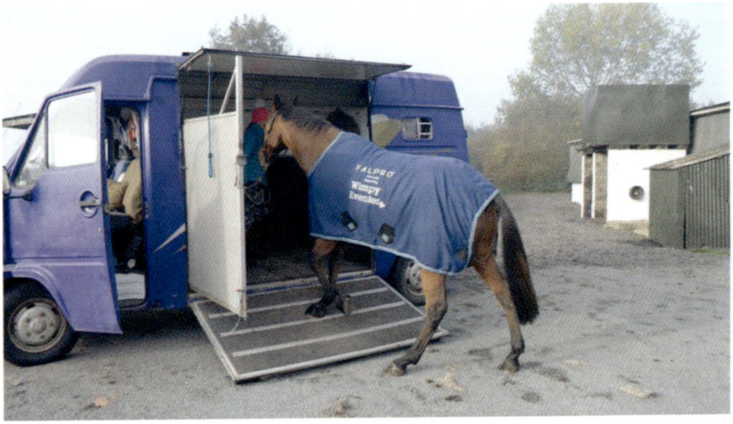
FALPRO
Wimpy
Eventer

Wimpy

PremBiz.co.uk
PremBiz

4

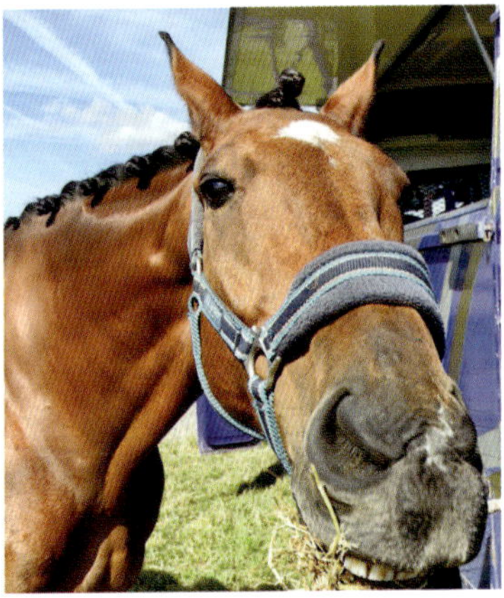

Whilst we are on a 'getting to know you' mission, I thought it might be fun to list 30 things you might not have known about me. Here goes...

1. Favourite smell? Hot horse, you know the sweaty smell after a jumping session or the smell of the steam in the air when you gather at a covert post gallop out hunting - that smell. Or cat paws, they smell a bit like popcorn.

2. Biggest fear? Losing the people I love. Hands down. I am sh*t scared when Pat bronchs with me but nothing comes close to this.

3. Favourite pizza? Black olive and Palma ham… I LOVE a thin crust too, none of that doughy stuff!

4. Favourite Flower? Honeysuckle or hydrangea, or Wisteria if I could get the bloody thing to grow!

5. Favourite breed of dog? Not a huge doggy person but I like the non-stinky kind!

6. Favourite place to visit? Christmas markets or my Mum and Dads for Sunday dinner!

7. Roller Coasters? Definitely not, maybe a steady log flume.

8. Favourite Ice Cream? Homemade (with far too much condensed milk), strawberry.

9. Pet peeve? Eating with your mouth open or hearing people being nasty about others. You know what? I'm not a Saint, I have said things about people I shouldn't have said and regretted it, but fess up. I've apologised to almost everyone that I've said anything mean about now, and it's a really great thing to do. Often, I find things get Chinese Whispered out of all reality, and

so if you haven't had my apology, I probably didn't say anything about you at all!

10. Shorts or jeans? I dislike both in equal measures, I'm a chino/legging or skirt person! Jeans make me feel FAT, they're restrictive and scratchy and I haven't found a pair that don't make me feel monstrously fat yet!

11. What are you listening to right now? My typing?! I'm writing a book if you hadn't noticed!

12. Colour of your vehicle? Pearlescent white!! Not just white… oh no, Alfa Romeo kindly named the dingey, off white of my cheap hatchback something far more fancy! – It's not fancy, it's dented and full of horse items that smell worse than Pat's show day excrement!

13. Colour of eyes? Green/hazel – Oh and while we're at it, I'm not naturally ginger. Mousey brown with notes of auburn but it's what suits me best I think and now I've got a f*ck ton of grey hairs, I will always colour it!!

14. Favourite Foods? Blue cheese, prosciutto, creme brûlée

15. Favourite Holiday? Seriously, anywhere with my Carrot that doesn't bankrupt us that is hot without too many flying insects. Ha ha ha… pretty much leaves us with Skegness for that one hot day of the British Summer then!

16. Night Owl or Day Person? Day, I can't stay up late… I'm nodding off on the sofa usually around 9pm.

17. Favourite day of the week? Saturday, oooo or maybe Friday afternoon. It's like, what do you prefer; Christmas Eve or Christmas Day… is the anticipation better than the actual?!

18. Do you have a nickname? Well, I'm almost certainly not a Vicky, it's just not my name!!! But Vic is fine and Wimpy has stuck now and I don't mind that either :)

19. Favourite Music? Dolly Parton

20. Tattoos? None! I don't like paying for pain.

21. Do you like to cook? Yes, very much.

22. Beer or Wine? Wine, but only good wine... a Chablis, Gavi, Rioja, Tempranillo, Marlborough, Malbec... I love good wine, but there isn't much I dislike more than bad wine!

23. How's your driving? Poor to reckless! Actually, I'd say pretty good. I used to drive a lot and I was very good, but now I'm motoring less, it's got a bit wayward!

24. Do you wear perfume? Yes, most days

25. If so, what kind? Lancôme, it's usually gifted.

26. Favourite colour? PINK!!! If you hadn't guessed.

27. Do you like vegetables? Yes, all of them I think!!

28. Do you work out? Never, apart from riding, the only exercise I do is walking to and opening the fridge!

29. Do you wear glasses? No but I definitely should.

30. Favourite season? Autumn or winter. I like wrapping up warm and I LOVE mulled wine, open fires, dark nights, big jumpers, fluffy socks… I'd sacrifice dry fields and clean horses for that any day!

**3 Fascinating Facts:**

I was runner up Miss Lincolnshire 2008

I have been on the X-Factor, didn't get on the telly though

I am absolutely terrified of the dentist and have to be sedated.

So, it's mid-December and Bender has been in the new yard for nearly a week. He's doing SO well and I might just be getting a little carried away, but…

I have just got all the dates in the diary for HOYS qualifiers! I mean, call me optimistic but, I don't see why this isn't something we should be aiming for. Everyone needs a goal, right? The Horse of the Year Show is something I have dreamed of for many years, and having always bought cheap ex-racers that haven't always been that well behaved or that well put together, I've never made it.

The HOYS qualifiers are all over the country and on writing them down I soon realised that I might need to take out a bank loan or seriously reconsider bringing my planned Lottery win forward by a few years! They start in April and run through to August, around one a month, but none of them very bloody local!

Just to add, we will be entering the SEIB Search For A Star Racehorse to Riding horse class, which is for anyone that owns a horse that has raced under rules in the UK and Ireland.

At this point, I didn't know what he would be like at a show, I didn't have any of the gear I needed and I also hadn't managed to canter a 20 meter circle or trot in a straight line yet but they were all forgotten when I visualised Bender and I in that big sparkly arena. Drummers playing us in and the music singing us into our final gallop down the long side. My Carrot on the side lines holding a fancy show rug embroidered with 'Team Bender' and me; smiling like an asylum escapee as the judge pulls us in in first place! I could see it now; Vic and Bender ROR champions, nothing else seemed to matter much.

**December 10th 2017**

Today has already been one of the happiest days ever. I've been feeling a bit groggy this week and with so much to do it was really not good timing.

I got up early and went for a frosty mooch on Pat around our favourite ride, losing almost 2 hours catching up on chit chat with Auntie Smurph, which always makes me happy. Then back for sausages and Christmas snuggles with my Carrot.

At 2pm we drove up to have my first ride on Bender in his new residence. He has been with Piers and his team at Willow Banks since last week and I am just utterly astounded at the difference in his manners in general.

Piers has been lunging him in the Pessoa, and really getting him working forward and round. I thought it was time to be the pilot in his new environment, and I can report that Bender went the best he has ever gone.

We just did a few circles in walk, trot AND canter, and my word... the softness, the ease of the canter which I haven't really worked on at all since I've had him. I could have cried with delight.

He felt so balanced and so relaxed, far more than Pat sometimes. He was lazy though and this was really hard to adjust for me. Pat is SO sharp of my leg, and I found this very exhausting indeed.

I can't tell you how happy I am though. I was truly in despair over his separation anxiety and I thought I had reached the end of the line, but all my worries have disappeared.

He isn't calling, napping, getting anxious in the stable even though he can't directly see another horse.

For anyone dealing with this awful issue with your horses, there is hope, there is happiness to be found, and today I am happier than I've been for ages knowing my horse is content and rideable.

Now for Lincoln Christmas market and a few mulled wines to celebrate.

Love always,

Vic, Pat and Bender

Xxx

~

The rest of December was a total mine field. I had to go away with work, and at this point I was still working pretty much full time, albeit from home, as a marketing manager for a group of construction companies. I also had 4 days working at Olympia horse show and I was seriously struggling to get all the book parcels out in time for the big (Santa) day. Being away and living out of a suitcase for over a week was beginning to take its toll on my emotions.

To add to this heart ache, whilst at Olympia my lovely, and last remaining, Granny died at her home back in Lincolnshire. I was taken aback. First the shock hits and then I was just beside myself with worry for my Mum. I cannot imagine how she must have felt only months after losing her younger sister, to have now lost her Mum too. I'll never forget either of those phone calls from my sister for as long as I live. We just sat, hundreds of miles apart and cried together for a while. It makes me realise how isolated I have made things for myself. I still feel so young and so little when things like that happen. I am the youngest of four, two boy and two girls, and they are all so strong and people I can really look up to. I'm the only one without children of my own too, and I think that changes things for you. I've always been the childish one, the 'not quite grown up' and I needed a cuddle from any of them right then. I wanted to be there for them too and be strong, but instead I sat in a corner of the Olympia stadium and cried into a bottle of bramble whisky.

I missed home, I missed my Carrot and my family, I missed my boys and my cats. Working for a living is exceptionally over rated. But it was just one more hotel, one more day, one more speech delivery, 3 more trains and I'd be home for Christmas.

This is the thing isn't it, when you feel like this? You have to work hard to have horses, you need to earn more money than if you didn't have them, and this was the sacrifice. Just keep smiling, keep upbeat and keep focusing on why we work hard. Dry the tears, have a glass of wine and remember that you get bugger all in this life unless you make sacrifices. **LESSON 3: YOU DON'T GET ANYWHERE WITHOUT SACRIFICES.**

Sometimes it might not seem fair. Often, I see people who don't go to work, that have so much money that they buy saddlecloths they will never use, or have 2 lorries and one just sits there all year doing nothing. But really what do we know about each person's individual's sacrifices? The answer is, nothing. From the outside looking in, I have these two lovely horses and loads of daylight hours in which to ride them, but I work hard for that. It's easy to look and judge, but the answer is that we are all on our own journeys, every one of us is different and have different things we must do to get the enjoyment from our lives. But I'll tell you something else, the wine you consume on a Friday night tastes SO much better if you've worked hard for it.

Chances are, if you are feeling restless about something in your life or somethings don't feel like they are going well, you just need to push a little bit harder. It will pay off, maybe not straight away, but it will in time.

**23rd December 2017**

I'm feeling nervous, apprehensive maybe... I haven't ridden for a little while now because of work and someone (my friend, Piers Warmoth) thinks he's a funny Christmas Cilla Black and is matchmaking Bender and I with the demon that is SHOW JUMPING.... tomorrow!!

Ho ho holy sh*t!!! Pass me the Imodium!

The support from Piers and his team at Willow Banks is just so overwhelming that I'm actually going to trust him and jump a whole course in fancy dress with my Bender! A course of poles on the ground is still a course, right?!

~

Now, the hard work I had put in to enable me to afford having this horse trained by Piers was making such a remarkable difference to his progress. There is no way in the world I would have got to this point alone, in my muddy field so soon. I mean, we would have got there, but not after 3 weeks! Now I know all those long hours away were worth it, even if I was totally staining my undies of the thought of it.

**The Christmas Show**

So, it's Christmas Eve and what better way to spend it than sitting on the toilet waiting to complete a round of show jumps on your ex-racehorse that has never jumped a course before...

I awoke early and went to visit the golden balls pony (Pat), who I wished was my trusted steed for this morning's events... alas it was Benders' turn to shine.

Having been coaxed into doing this only yesterday by Piers, I took his word that death was far from imminent, and off we went.

I nervously tacked up my unflappable thoroughbred only three months into his retraining and mounted him for the first time in 10 days! I felt instantly at ease with my Carrot by my side and bobbled about the warm up avoiding the jumps.

Now, I have jumped Bender once in the field and he had a little pop on Thursday this week, but this is as far as his training has gone. So I entered the 30cms class.

He went in and jumped every single one in his half-arsed style, but we got our first ever first place rosette!!!! And I have to say, 30cms or not I felt like I'd just gone around Badminton, my beautiful bold boy jumped all those jumps for me.

I did eventually manage to jump something more than a leaf in the warm up and decided to enter the next class at 65cms.

We went in and did a very stylish clear and mostly in canter too! I was bursting with pride hearing our names read out in FIRST place AGAIN! Seriously, I've never had such a lovely time with a monstrously green horse on Christmas Eve! He tried so hard, coped so well in the warm up and gave me a lovely feeling over a jump too, I cannot ask for more.

Huge thank you to Piers and his team at Willow Banks and to all of you for your endless support. I'm also ever so lucky that my Voltaire Design saddle fits Pat and Bender, because I stuck to it like glue today.

What a day. What a horse. What a happy girl and her beautiful boys.

~

Whether Bender was in fact ready for this show or not, the reality is, I just got on with it. He went into the ring alone, didn't fuss about leaving the other horses behind in the warm up and he gave me the best Christmas gift ever. I don't think I have felt such joy for a long time and my hopes of HOYS were edging ever so slightly closer even if it was all costing me a lot of money.

**New Years Eve 2017**

I can't help but feel a little bit sad about this brilliant, brilliant year being over tonight.

Pat and I started the year determined to be the best we could be, and today we will end on some fun 80cm show jumping and pairs relay with Auntie Smurph.

Sadly, today was a day for survival, and I can't help but feel a little bit sad at how desperately scared I was again.

Pat was monstrously fresh when I got into the warm up, and all those demons came back to get me. I couldn't put my leg on, he bronched with me, and I almost went flying twice before I anchored myself down with my neck strap. He hasn't done that for months, and it's purely down to excitement that boils over. I can honestly say that it totally f*cking terrifies me. He is so short coupled that when he balls up like that you are literally sat on NOTHING!! I wanted to cry. But that was the first time he's been out to a jumping show since Norton Disney at the end of October, so I should have seen it coming.

We eventually got warmed up and settled and jumped a lovely round over the 80cms for 4 faults, due to a momentary blip where he just didn't appear to take off, and I ended up almost on the floor!

He was the quickest 4 faulter in a big class though, and we got 6th place!

Auntie Smurph and I then went back in for the pairs relay and came 3rd with 2 super-duper clears. This was SO much fun!

I feel like both Pat and I have gone back a few steps in confidence so lots of outings in the new year planned before we get back out on BE adventures again!

I feel also feel a bit sad that I close the doors on this truly amazing year, one that has been the absolute making of me and my horse.

- We went from be80 to be100 and cleared jumps over 1.10m!! I never imagined that this time last year I'd have done anything like I've done 2017. I couldn't even visualise getting on him without breaking into a sweat.
- I have self-published TWO books, and we have posted out over 9000 orders from our sitting room floor!
- We relocated 200 miles north and I now have my own business!
- I have now got my own column in a national magazine, Horse and Rider.
- Most importantly of all, I have grown as a person, I had goals and dreams, and I fought some huge battles to achieve them.

If you have a goal even just a tiny one, write it down NOW. You can do ANYTHING you set your heart and mind to. Trust me, you can.

I'd like to take this opportunity to thank you all for your endless support, for your motivation to keep going when I'm at rock bottom. YOU are the reason I have succeeded, and I will be eternally grateful.

Here's to making a life to be proud of in 2018

## January 2018

## Goal Setting

Oh January! You get me so full of hope and motivation to make myself thinner, richer, more successful and actually stop drinking my body weight in wine every week. This January was no different. I had decided to take on DRY JANUARY, where stupid people like to cease all alcohol consumption in order to act the smug ba*stard to all of their mates. I was fully intending to break my challenge by week 2 but my Mum always told me; "It's the taking part that counts." And there I was, sober as a judge for over two weeks!!! I get it, you might think I'm a little dependent on booze by now, and I might well be. But Friday night, when you've worked your arse off all week, you just want 3 glasses of wine as a reward… is that so bad?! It's not like I'm drinking Tesco's own brand whisky from a brown paper bag on a Tuesday morning. – Now there's a New Year's Resolution if ever I saw one!!!

So, the new year started just as I had planned. I set out with a plan for this year, to get Bender to HOYS and Pat qualified for the Badminton Grassroots 2019 or, at the very least, a couple of Regional Final tickets. I had mapped out my season and realised I was going to have to work my fingers to the bone for it to happen.

And that's right about where the wheels fell off!

**15th January 2018**

Today is Friday. I have been away since Wednesday morning, not ridden Bender since Tuesday or Pat since Sunday... the motivated start to my new year is NOT going well!

I have today and tomorrow morning and we're off again back down to London this weekend. These are things I cannot get out of and it's making me feel that sense of guilt creeping in.

Motivation is a funny thing, I can feel totally powered up and ready to go when there's no chance of me being able to knuckle down! But chances are, when I can... I won't want it half as much enthusiasm!

Today is actioning day!

I am desperate to raise the remaining money for my lorry now. Visualising having him sat on the drive or being able to get in him and have my own freedom to pop to the beach on an afternoon would just make me so happy. Never mind save me £160 on my event cost every time!

So what needs to change? Bender will be coming out of full livery. This has served a brilliant purpose of weaning them off each other and getting him going in the arena but I have to think about the long term goals. The lorry will progress him more than another 3 months in livery will, I'm sure.

Budgeting; I'm going to write down ALL of my income and outgoings and strip everything back. I need to know where every penny is going so that I can go to shows as well as save for my lorry.

So, I've written it all down. I feel more motivated already, grabbing life by the horns today and getting stuff done.

And just remember; you are on your own journey, no one else's. Live a life of being true to who you really are inside, be kind and you will always have people who love you.

Have the most wonderful weekend, make sure you laugh often, enjoy the moments that matter and squeeze a pony or two. Fill your heart with love and it will radiate from your face like the toasty glow of a log fire! Enjoy it.

Love as always Vic xxxxx

~

Having ridden Bender a few more times at Willow Banks and made the decision that we might be ready to cope on our own, I decided to move him off full livery. I also chose not to move him back home straight away because it was royally muddy, and I really needed an arena to ride him in, so we could keep things consistent.

I found a lovely little DIY yard with an arena around 11 miles away. This seemed doable, and I moved him there the following week. He settled so well and despite them having limited turnout, he was amazingly calm and just as good to ride as he was at the other place.

On that subject; I want to talk about retraining.

I'll add right now, I am NO expert, but I do have experience and I'm not afraid to use it!

So, you have a horse that has inevitably learnt to go a certain way, who favours right over left, head in the air over round and soft. He wants to run through the bridle when you put your leg on or spooks constantly and has zero trust in you… any of this sounding familiar?

Now I don't know if I have just got unlucky but all 4 horses that I have owned have all had bad habits, learned from a previous way of going.

**Horse 1 – India** 4yo thoroughbred mare: Bought out of NH training and had a flighty nature. She was a feisty, hard mouthed 4 year old that took my very last nerve to re-educate. Her problems were purely inexperience and age related but nonetheless, I had a tough gig for my first horse.

**Horse 2 – Freckles** 4yo warmblood gelding: Bought as a very green baby and he had dreadful issues almost resembling agoraphobia. The further we got away from home the higher and further over he reared, this was again down to inexperience and age but not great learned behaviour that I had a job fixing.

**Horse 3 – Pat** 5yo thoroughbred x Irish draught gelding: Pat had fear seeping out of his skin, he was scared of everything and wouldn't take any kind of contact in the reins without dipping behind the bridle. Team this with the sensitivity and sharp nature, and I had a ticking bomb under me many times!

**Horse 4 – Bender** 7yo thoroughbred gelding: Bender is probably the easiest of the bunch, but his separation anxiety is probably the worst I have come across in all of the 500 horses I have looked after in the last 20 years.

Now, each one had something to work on and all of them had the potential to get better and be wonderful. I was trained from 7 years old (that's 25 years now) by some of the country's most practical horsemen and women, using traditional methods that I know work. And I know they work because with each of these horses, the same theory has improved each one.

**Good Groundwork – is ESSENTIAL.**

Lunging, long reining, leading, tying up, rugging, grooming, loading. MANNERS are vital. Don't let him bite you, head butt you, pull you over, etc. I can't think of anything that I find more frustrating than seeing someone get dragged around by their horse, it's not fun and it's certainly not safe.

Gain respect without fear and you've got trust.

That comes from good rules on the floor. Teach him to back up, to stand and lead nicely. It might take months, but you'll have years of enjoyment in return. Repetition is key, do things over and over until they are so boring you want to stick pins in your eyes.

Know when it's time to get on; there is a pivotal point in the groundwork training where the trust is established enough to have a good, safe first ride. I won't mount until that point – it could be a week, it could be 3 months. But don't rush it. What's the rush anyway?! You'll have gained respect and trust on the ground that will make mounting your horse safe and isn't that what you want?

**Ridden work – basic, solid footings.**

Don't over complicate things, if it's not working do something else. Have eyes on the ground at least once a month from someone you trust to set you straight (no one is right all the time!).

Think about 3 things;

1. STOP: vocally during groundwork you will have used a command that will aid the stopping when things are getting a bit onward. It's that simple make sure stop and rest commands work before you kick on.

2. GO: don't just kick! You might be launched into next week, you've earned the trust - use it. Be vocal. Daddy Carrot is learning voice commands with Bender and does a very good woman's voice for 'walk on'!

3. Steering: well, more flexion and getting the horse to use his abdominal muscles. It's key to getting control of their whole body and having them use themselves correctly. Once they learn to bend around your leg and lift up their big barrel bellies, you'll find the neck drops, the frame relaxes, and you don't fight for an 'outline'. Having control of their body means you also have a fall back if things don't go as you planned, move the body to break the naughtiness, simple right?

And that's just it, keep it simple one thing at a time. Repeat things often and don't lost patience. It might take your brain a second to process something, but a horse is 8 times your size with a walnut for a brain…. remember that when things aren't going how you thought they would.

You'll also find, if you're focussing hard enough on correct training, every ounce of fear you ever had just evaporates. Yes, I still get flutters of racing heart but, believe what you are doing is correct, don't be afraid to ask for the right kind of help and stick two fingers up to people who look at you like you've got 'Tw*t' marker penned across your forehead. You'll show them.

Enjoy your horses, first and foremost. Cross stitch feels very under rated when you're getting hauled through a hedge by a bolshy beast!

~

**10th January 2018**

7 weeks on Saturday ladies and gentlemen... 7 little tiny, tiny weeks.

The countdown is on and I need to tick off the following before then;

XC training

Set up my field arena

Jump at least once a week

Hack three times a week

Sort out my calmer doses so I don't die

Save money for entry fees

Find my balls

Clip off remaining fur!

Lose a stone or buy new breeches!

I could go on but it's just terrifying! Gearing up and getting in the zone is hard enough but it doesn't feel five minutes since the 2017 season finished.

First event will be Epworth BE90 (or 80, I haven't decided quite yet!).

It's hard to keep a focus when there are SO many things to focus on! I read something somewhere that it's Blue Monday coming up too, this is meant to be the most depressing day of the year. Everyone's skint, the daylight hours are giving everyone SAD and you can't see light at the end of the dark January tunnel. – I'll be looking forward to that!

I don't think I dislike January as such, it's not poor January's fault you can't get your arse in gear! But I do want to say a big, fat, hairy 'B*llocks' to Blue Monday!

Let's roll back 18 months; It was a balmy late August evening when I finally located enough of my own hairy balls to get on and go for a ride outside of a confined area for the first time in a while. I slugged hard on my hip flask and led my half-doped horse out of the stable.

Trembling at the knees and sweating in the palms, I lugged my fat backside onto the sticky gel seat-saver and off we went. I think I had reached the 1/2 mile point before I dared to release the death grip, I had on the neck strap in order to light my cigarette.

I exhaled a huge cloud of smoke and port fumes and finally relaxed to about 65% of what was my natural state. I trotted for a while and edged into a small canter on the verge. It felt amazing, all those feelings of failure and guilt of 'not doing' melted away, and there I was, 'doing' for the first time in ages.

I came home a short while later and untacked my horse, I slumped into the corner of the stable and cried. Not tears of sadness, but tears of relief, utter relief that I wasn't a failure, that I could do something despite the fear.

There it was; the realisation that fear doesn't have to win.

Fear causes mental blockages that I now know can be unblocked. The paralysis, the sweating, the 'not doing', these are all things YOU CAN control.

So big hairy goat b*llocks to you Blue Monday, because I'm better than feeling sorry for myself these days, I'm better than dwelling on the negatives, I'm a fear fighter and I'm doing alright!

~

I was doing alright, looking back can often make you see how far it is you've come. Don't be afraid to look back. Pat and I have a lot of history. Some of it isn't stuff I want to remember, but doing so, I feel like we are getting somewhere and not just spiralling into more darkness. I think it is much harder to gauge when you are head over heels in love with your horse too. He was like the leather jacket wearing, motorbike riding, spunky boyfriend that I probably should have steered away from… but that's my Carrot in a nutshell too! I am my own undoing!

And on that front, since moving back to Lincolnshire in July, having a lovely Christmas in our new home and feeling much more content, our marriage was as strong as an ox. It's very important to have an ally to tell everything to, one that doesn't judge you despite the (often) bad decisions you make, and one that will help you pick up your last scraps of dignity without belittling you. It took me until I was 27 to find him, I married the wrong one first time around and had a fair few wrong ones in the middle, but I got there. I do think there is someone out there for everyone and it might be that they're right in front of you and you just haven't noticed yet?

~

Now, as the January days slip away, I am driving 44 miles a day just do go and do Bender on DIY, and it's becoming increasingly difficult to keep both horses going. My confidence is in tatters after one bad ride.

I stupidly got on Bender In. A. Bad. Mood. This is always a BIG mistake but what made it worse was that Bender, for the first time, properly got the hump with me. After 10 minutes I ended up getting off before I knocked ten bells of sh*t out of him. I was angry that he felt wooden, I was frustrated that he couldn't pick up left canter after how hard I'd been working on it. I was raging that I couldn't get a tune out of him and NONE of this was HIS fault. It was all mine. The cracks were staring to show.

Days like that, you should NEVER get on a horse, never mind one that needs hand holding or training. But I did, I'm not perfect!

I then spent the next few days resenting him and the time I spent over there trying to form a bond, whilst Pat was playing the lead part in 'Feral Beryl the Musical' at home. Since I moved him to the DIY yard, I had spent over 2 hours every day fussing with him and grooming him, in some kind of hope that I would find the connection like I had with Pat. I didn't feel happy around him very often and this was making things very hard all round.

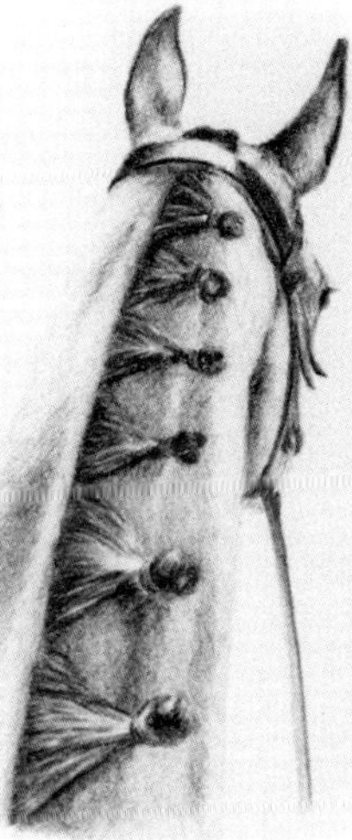

## February 2018

## Stripped back

I was finding things all a bit too much, and I was massively running short of money having entered early (so I didn't back out); Pat's first two events at Epworth and Oasby, in March. What with the livery and fuel and time away from working to spend with Bender at the other yard, I was running myself ragged and skint!

In need of some kind of solace, I went to Pilates for the first time. Now, I'm not one for communal exercising of any kind, but this was so relieving of my anxiety. I found it really cleansing and I felt very emotionally balanced every time I came out of that musty smelling village hall. It was during one particular Pilates session that I laid on my borrowed mat and had a moment of total clarity.

In my head someone asked me; *Are you enjoying these horses?* – My reply was, No. They asked if I have ever enjoyed Bender at all and again, apart from the two rides at Willow Banks over Christmas, I hadn't enjoyed him at all. He was breaking my heart. I wanted to love him, and I wanted him to fit in, but he didn't. So, on 9th February 2018 I wrote this;

Do you solemnly declare to tell the truth? The whole truth? And nothing but the truth?

I do.

I'm not coping.

Not at all.

Here it is; the saddest and most heartfelt post I think I have ever written down.

My nerves are trashed, totally frayed. And not just riding, which is the saddest part of all. I'm lost. I've been getting very upset almost every day for the last 2 weeks and the pressure I have felt has been incredible.

I am exhausted, I'm working very hard at work to keep money rolling in, but having the two horses and in particular Bender who is totally breaking my heart, is the cause of most of this sadness.

He is the sweetest, most affectionate horse, and I've been trying everything to form a bond with him, but it's not working. Every day I have spent hours with him, we don't work together, and I don't know why. He was lovely for Piers at Willow Banks and never put a little hoof out of line, but he senses my insecurities and I can't fix them. Left alone, I am causing him to feel insecure too, and it's breaking my heart every day.

I know if someone came to me with this message, I would say that life is too short to be so unhappy. Horses are my hobby and when they make other areas of your life sad, you should look at resolving it before you spiral down that dark road again.

Pat and I just get each other, he looks to me for leadership and I can give him it, I look to him for comfort and he gives me that in return. We are best friends. And I'm destroyed that I can't find even a glimmer of hope with Bender.

This isn't a decision I have made lightly, and I am thoroughly expecting a whole world of disappointment from people that wanted to see us do well. I'm sorry. I do feel a let-down, I've let him down too.

I need to find him someone that will love him, continue his training and give him what he needs. He is a beautiful horse and will make someone so very happy.

I really am sorry.

I know that this is the best thing for the horse and that is, and always will be, my main priority.

Reality hurts more than ever now that I've opened the wound for everyone to see.

For anyone else, in any 'normal' situation, I don't expect they would feel as though they have to justify themselves all the b*stard time like I do. When I make a decision like this, I don't just feel as though it's me I am letting down.

There were so many people that wished us well, that were rooting for us to go to HOYS, that sent messages and wrote comments of support. I just felt like a total f*cking let down. And of course, no-one voiced that. I was already broken enough, but I tortured myself about it for days afterwards. I knew that I wouldn't want to go up there at all now I had made the decision. But it was a new day, the plaster was torn off and now I had to find my boy the very best home possible.

His advert was also quite hard to write because I didn't want much money for him, only the best home. This can sometimes bring with it; joy riders, inexperienced people or ones that won't have the money to look after him properly. I'd had him for 6 months, during that time we had established that he is a much happier horse in a bigger yard not just in a pair where he can get quite clingy. That type of living arrangement probably wasn't going to be free, the buyer needed to be the right one.

He had had a year off before coming to me, so I'd spent 2-3 months long-reining and in hand manners training before getting on. He had a very lazy disposition but was NOT confident hacking alone with me. This is where we hit a brick wall I think. He would long rein on his own, so it was likely to be my nerves making this an issue.

He absolutely loved jumping though, and didn't spook at any fillers, he wasn't silly in the warm up at the show and was an angel in the ring. But his new Mum or Dad would need to be able to kick as he wasn't a speedy Gonzales!

What I was looking for was someone that had a good knowledge and empathy, that was looking for a partner to love and cuddle. – This might be harder than I thought.

~

Over the next two weeks I kept him ticking over as the first buyers were set to visit. They came and rode him, and he went so beautifully that I felt like retracting everything I said and keeping him after all. I hadn't ever seen anyone on him and he looked amazing for the lady that day. I drove home so seriously confused and unhappy about my decisions and just hoped they would come and take him before I changed my mind.

They arranged a 5 stage vetting using a vet they chose all the way from Cheshire. It was such a windy day and I totally bottled out riding him for the vet. It became very obvious how much my confidence had been dented just lately. I was full of fear yet again, something else that was making me feel like utter crap, never mind the guilt of selling him.

I recognised that anxiety creeping in again.

I felt it badly when I left the house one day that vetting week. I was meant to be driving down to West Sussex for work and I had already cried that morning when Gary left for work, not at all like me. I got in the car and went to do Pat, then to Bender. Getting on the road about 11am and just 20 minutes into the journey I had pulled onto the hard shoulder. I sat and cried so hard into my scarf I thought my head was going to explode.

I couldn't cope; with the drive, with the vetting, with work, with anything. I felt truly desolate for the first time in years. I thought I had a handle on this now, I thought I was okay. I was meant to be fine now we moved to Lincolnshire. I was not fine.

I felt sick, I felt empty inside. I would never say that I felt suicidal, but I felt nothing for life. I called the doctor right there on the side of the road. I needed to talk to someone, someone who didn't know me.

I explained to the lady on reception that I needed to speak to a doctor who called me back within 10 minutes. I told her how I was feeling and where I was and what I was meant to be doing. I didn't even feel stupid, I didn't feel a burden either, because I knew I needed them to help me. I took the advice I was given and drove home.

I attended an appointment the following day and talked through all of it again. I cried a lot, but I felt so much better for letting it all out. That's the thing with mental health you see; the more you ignore it the worse it gets. Never ignore a niggle. Recognise when something isn't right. I wish I had done something sooner, I hadn't been feeling right for a little while.

I went down the homeopathic route (due to us trying to conceive) and started taking a high dosage of St. John's Wort. I do get that this might not be the most effective way, but I was happy with the decision and within 2 weeks I was like a totally different person. I don't know whether it was the remedy or the fact that I had got it all off my chest, but I felt like me again, full of life and ready to get going.

And yes, you read it right; Conceive! I might not have mentioned this to date because, you know… some things are private. But we've come this far together, I have nothing to hide from you.

In September/October time we made the decision not to renew my next contraceptive injection, and do, what we like to call; 'not, not try'. Keeping things very nonchalant, and if it happened then GREAT and if not, we wouldn't be too worried about it.

In hindsight, I should have put two and two together because that imbalance of hormones hit me harder than I ever thought possible. I felt like a totally different person, and the withdrawal from this drug I had been injecting into myself for 3 years, was probably the culprit of my breakdown in mental stability at that time.

**9th February 2018**

Anxiety and hormones, go on... F*ck off!!!

(Sorry gents!)

So here it is, another brazenly honest word vomit...

I'm struggling. Still. I know, I know... she's always f*cking moaning about something but here's the thing; it's effected my whole life and I want people to know that this sh*t is normal!

In November I released my body from any kind of chemical contraception. Prior to that I was injected 4 times a year so that we could carry out exercise of the horizontal kind without fear of producing a sizeable litter. (Sorry mum, **I have sex**, there I said it!)

So, December I felt fine, but two weeks into January, and I was not at all fine. I have felt sad often, cried often, felt worthless, lifeless and unmotivated. It totally spiralled out of control.

Now, I'm never hormonal or a sobber so I knew this wasn't me. I literally wanted to go f*cking crazy at people for no reason what so ever. Scream at people for doing things that pissed me off, where normally I'd let them wash over me! I cried for three days in a row over absolutely nothing, I couldn't tell you what I was sad about. I was just heart wrenchingly unhappy.

I made everything into a problem to the point where, for almost a week, I hibernated with the curtains shut so I didn't have to face life. It's reality and it hurts to even talk about it.

I have turned a corner in the last 10 days, I have picked myself up with the help of St. John's Wort on recommendation of the doctor. But here's the thing;

HY
ONIT
HY

BRAVE

Don't ever feel alone.

Ever.

Promise me right now. Because it's just horrible. If ANYONE reading this ever feels sad and alone, you come to me. I've felt very alone these last few weeks and although I'm bettering these feelings every day, I want people to know that this is real f*cking life, and you WILL feel better soon.

I love you all very much

Vic

xxx

Please don't ever suffer alone. Promise me.

~

Now, where was I? Ahh yes…

Bender was so lovely that week and I even had a jump on him in the school which was very bittersweet! And I was about to realise that fate has a very funny way of telling you something wasn't meant to be.

He didn't pass the vetting.

He had a few weakness related issues that may or may not be a problem later on in his life. Bla…bla… bla…!

Seriously, my blood boils for this subject.

I have NEVER had a horse vetted in my life, granted I have never spent that much money on horses, and they have always been bought more as pets than investments, but;

**NUMBER 1**: the horse has no concept of its value. It could just as likely injure itself in the lorry picking it up than have some long-standing degenerative disease. You shouldn't gamble all your money on a horse. Ask yourself; "can I afford to write off the purchase price?" if not, seriously reconsider the purchase until you can. They are animals with feelings, nerves, muscles, bones and tendons. They also have a 500kg body and a walnut sized brain… you do the maths!

**NUMBER 2**: If you cannot tell a horse is sound when you try it, you should be taking someone who can tell, or reconsidering your animal purchase. Lame hamsters are much less heartache.

**NUMBER 3:** If you need to get anything done, get bloods and x-rays. Cold hard facts. Failing flexion tests do not mean the horse won't come to anything. There are several top Olympic horses that have failed a flexion test on an off day in their careers.

I feel quite strongly about this topic because a very good friend of mine had a horse vetted by a qualified and practicing horse vet, who turned out was embroiled in the most revolting scam with a couple of horse dealers. There were horses with feet glued together, hidden ailments, fake passports, broken and fused bones; most were injected up to their eyeballs with enough cortisone and steroid to numb a rhino, just to mask the pain for prospective buyers. It was DISGUSTING and from that day I have never taken any notice. You must be knowledgeable enough to know that something isn't right and as I said, if you're not, just find someone you trust that is.

Anyway, the prospective buyer pulled out, there and then. And I do understand. Sometimes you might not have the money if it did go wrong, but I felt sad for him too, it would have been a lovely home.

So, February was turning into a bit of cruddy old month! I felt like burying my head in the sand and calling time on this whole horse thing! I had some nasty comments on social media again too, something that I thought I was dealing with quite well, but I just took something to heart about my riding and my intentions, meaning things weren't improving on the mood front either.

Yet again, I let fear and insecurity take a hold of my life.

**16th February 2018**

What a week, not at all the one I expected to have

So here it is, I've withdrawn from Epworth and Oasby. I know what you're all thinking, and you're probably half right. But the truth is, I'm not ready to do it yet, and I'm not going out there half-hearted and ruining my horse's confidence because mine isn't intact.

My first BE event will be the BE80 at Norton Disney in April (my birthday weekend). So, with that in mind, and not one to dwell for too long…

Tonight, I am heading to Hartpury for the Mary King demo and doing a takeover on Instagram for Horse&Rider Magazine! I'm hoping to leave feeling mightily inspired and ready to take this season on!

Funny thing about this Wimpy world I have created, I don't always want to live in it and sometimes I forget how judgemental others can be.

I just want to make sure no one ever has to feel like they are worthless because of what people say on the internet, or anywhere else. It's just not fair. These people wouldn't come to my house, knock on my door and say it to my face. They wouldn't f*cking dare! They are actually insecure cowards deep down.

If ever you feel like sh*t because of a comment on the internet, just stop and think how sad they must be for doing it in the first place. I will support you, without judging or demoralising you.

The love and kindness shown by people in the Wimpy community must be celebrated. We must build each other up to help us reach those dreams. Make equestrianism a sport of support and friendship for a common love of our horses.

F*cksake, I'm not asking for world peace or the end to global suffering. I'm just asking that people refrain from tearing strips off one another for wearing the wrong shade of turquoise numnah!

Think before you speak, think about how you might feel. Give people the benefit of the doubt, perhaps they just need help or advice instead of berating. Keep that in mind when you hear gossip too, correct people, be a voice of reason and don't just join in a crowd of bullies.

Isn't it a nice feeling to be nice, to say something kind? To help someone when they feel sad? It's a much nicer one than the sour taste of putting them down.

Don't worry about being the person you truly are at the fear of being labelled 'different', I'm sure Mary King isn't worried when she's out there being amazing!!

~

I had the most amazing time at Hartpury. I went with my friend Dave and, despite us getting a little bit lost on the way, he bought me KFC for tea and were weren't late after all.

In the break, I took the brazen, but opportune moment to accost poor Mrs King. I grabbed my baby pink and blue hat silk from the car and, like an over e-numbered toddler, I ran and knocked on her lorry door.

What the f*ck I thought I was doing, I don't know. But, with my Sharpie in hand, she welcomed me in, finished necking her Peroni and signed my hat silk. RESULT!

I literally couldn't believe I was standing there in her lorry whilst she drank a beer. I'd loved to have shared one with her, but alas, I was merely some marker pen wielding groupie encroaching on her bevvy.

I left graciously, and to this day, I will never forget meeting the person that I had spent years gazing at on my bedroom wall posters, in a wet carpark in Gloucestershire (at the age of 31 and 3 quarters!).

~

Back home and hitting reality with a bump, I had a few messages about Bender and followed a couple of them up. One was from a lovely local lady who had a yard not that far away, and who I knew was VERY experienced. We spoke on the phone and she really liked him from the videos. I also explained that my confidence wasn't great, and that I didn't want to look like a bumbling buffoon showing him off for her, which she was very kind about indeed. That weekend, she picked him up. Only on a trial basis, but I knew she would love him and do her best for him. I wrote the money off there and then if I'm honest. I wanted him to have a good home, and if that meant that she didn't feel like she could gamble on him financially, I was okay with that. His happiness was worth more to me than money.

I received regular Bender updates for the next few weeks. Videos of him hacking out on his own down the road made me smile the most. Sometimes, some horses just aren't for you. That was us. He was settled and took everything in his stride and I don't think his new mum would be bringing him back in a hurry!

Not forgetting, in the middle of all of this was little Pat. Who had a seasons eventing ahead of him, and who hadn't been ridden for nearly two whole weeks, it was far from ideal! The DIY yard I had kept Bender on was paid up until the first week of March, so

I decided to use this as a kick start for Pat. I shipped him into the space and began knuckling down to business.

**18th February 2018**

I'm on cloud nine...

Yesterday I moved Pat with the help of lovely Auntie Smurph and we now have an enclosed space in which to get my confidence back.

Part of my Horse&Rider Magazine contract is a monthly video of us tackling some of the magazine exercises and today, we had filming to do.

Wait for it....

I THINK I FLOATED OFF TO HEAVEN!

After almost two weeks off, I thought he would come out a little stiffy plank but, boy was I wrong. He went the absolute best he's gone in the whole 6.5 years I've had him!

I didn't do much, and some people will probably roll their eyes about the sheer delight without rosettes or jumps involved, but he was unbelievable today.

We trotted about a bit, did some transitions and then I offered him the rein for a stretch... well.... my neck strap slipped up to his ears he was so low.

It's the best feeling in the world being on a happy, stretchy, swinging horse that's glistening underneath you. I'm struggling to put it into words how happy I felt. Just did 30 minutes of flatwork but I didn't actually want to get down. I rarely feel like that, hardly ever these days and I am moist in the eye area feeling it once more.

Anything is possible.

~

Turns out, having daily access to an arena for the first time in months was actually doing us the world of good. I still maintain that I am better off without one, so that I'm forced to hack (which I am distinctly more scared of) and not just ride in the comfort of an enclosed space. But there are some things that you cannot do in a field in winter when you work for a living and don't have flood lights! I was buzzing to get up there and ride him every day, just because it was a novelty and I wasn't used to it, I guess – something I definitely used to take for granted.

Having this safe arena space and jumps, also meant I was getting my confidence back in bucketful's, and the change in Pat was very noticeable too.

## March 2018

## It's all coming up a bit soon!

You know sometimes, when you sit and think for too long, you talk yourself in and out of decisions? You feel confused and need guidance on which way to turn?

The decision to leave that job you hate, to get married, to start a family, to try something that has an end result that is out of your control.

It leaves a seed (or boulder) of doubt or uncertainty lurking around. That is inevitable and anyone that tells you otherwise is bolder than the boulder itself.

My battle with fear has taken on many forms this year, and it was only March. My main concern used to be a fear of f*cking up, of disappointing people and not doing as well as I know I can. Now I couldn't give two sh*ts about ballsing it up. I'm now scared of hurting myself, more than I ever have been. I'm scared I might fall off, that I might hurt myself or that Pat might run off and get hit by a car.

But, here's the reality.

The bottom line is; with horses, **YOU WILL NEVER BE 100% IN CONTROL**. Unless they're dead or heavily sedated! You must learn a way of embracing that feeling of being a little bit out of control and I had mastered that last year. I loved galloping in a big field I LOVED it, so that's what I need to do. Learn to love being a little bit out of control again.

Fear takes many forms and it changes faces often too, rationalise what it is you are actually afraid of and deal with it, don't let it rule your life.

Don't let fear be the reason you didn't take that opportunity, enter that show, marry that person... who knows, sticking a finger up to fear might just be the best thing you've ever done!

You see, I am scared. But I'm doing it anyway. And regardless of that fear, I will continue to do it until I don't feel so scared anymore. I think that's the only way if you're too stubborn to give up, like me!

Once, I actually said it out loud. Addressing my spooky, fresh horse; "Please don't do that, you're frightening me!!" He didn't reply, obviously! But I didn't feel in control and that's what I was most scared of. I felt like, at any minute, I could have fallen off.

And that's when it hit me; Do you know how many times in the last 7 years of having Pat, that I have actually fallen off….?

TWICE. Two times. Just 2 falls in 7 years. And before that, I think I fell off maybe 3 or 4 times in total since I was 22 and owned my own horses. Crikey, growing up I fell off a lot, but that's how you learn to stay on, and how you teach yourself to be balanced and ready for anything. I do feel ready and I do feel balanced, I just need reminding that I'm good enough sometimes. I'm realising that this is definitely a battle of confidence and not skill that I'm fighting.

**Remember: Knowledge is Power.**

Back to March, and the early spring SNOW had arrived! Yep, it came just in time to f*ck up my pre-season training and leave my horse standing in his stable for days. Pat is not great being cooped up, and starts getting restless, very sharp to ride and not great to deal with in general. Queue March disaster number 1:

**8th March 2018**

The little sh*t escaped! Yep, that's right … he was tied up outside his stable being skipped out when I wasn't there, and he pulled back and buggered off!

This snow has an awful lot to answer for I can tell you!

~

Over the next few days, I was able to give him a lunge in the small indoor school at the DIY yard, and when I eventually got to ride him again, I had ended up getting off far sooner than planned and not as a result of pant stains!

Pat was very tight, more spooky, crabby, a bit bucky and guarded in his movement and just not himself. I hadn't pushed him because it had been desperately out of character, and I felt as though he was trying to tell me something.

I decided to bring him back home to the field ASAP and back on 24/7 turnout which I was convinced would help him feel better. Lord knows the event season is starting for most people and mine should be too, in just 3 weeks! It wasn't looking hopeful!

~

By the time I got him home, he was back to his jolly self and I was so relieved. He hadn't had a significant amount of down time either which meant that he wasn't exactly lacking in fitness to wobble us around a BE80. It was competition practice I was lacking and so instead of going straight out to do an affiliated event in April, this happened:

**22nd March 2017**

The balance of fear and doing...

I've just done something really, bloody stupid! I've entered a 'pre-event'!

So, I was feeling desperately unprepared for my first BE event on the 7th April, so what do I do? Enter an unaffiliated one for the 1st. April Bloody Fool! I'll be the only one looking a fool I can tell you!

I'm calling it a practice run. Most local XC schooling venues have events on at weekends now, so they aren't available for plopping round as practice. I'm using this as my practice! – Ever the prepared pilot.

I've been to the toilet twice since registering my interest, but I just don't want to feel like this anymore. I'm sick of being beaten by nerves. And the only way to banish them is DOING it!

I'm going in with no expectations, no pressure and hopefully no vomit on my shirt! I'm doing the smallest height they had available too, so I can just get over this total gut-wrenching dread I have developed over the winter.

I know that so many of us feel like this, I question often if it's all worth it. So, I leave you with this…

My first event of last season was a year ago this weekend. I was SERIOUSLY frightened, in fact, I nearly followed through waiting for Carrot to get his morning coffee! But, I got on and rode the dressage, and then got back on and did the jumping and if that wasn't enough, I got on a third time and nailed the cross country. You can do things even if you're scared. That is a FACT.

There's the focus, the determination epicentre.

Let's do this!!!!

~

Best thing really!

I'd had Pat back in the field on the farm near our house for just over a week before I started feeling much more myself! We hacked every day possible and I also did some pole work in our squidgy field. I would just walk down to him with a brush and my saddle and clamber on from the hay feeder. It might not sound much, but I felt very chuffed with my change in confidence and progress as the season was eking ever closer.

**25th March 2017**

Yesterday, after a shove from Auntie Smurph on the way home from her show, I booked into two dressage tests for today at Hill House Equestrian.

Two novice tests, and to be brutally honest, I didn't care which tests they were. I didn't care if I came last in each class or did a 20% test, I just wanted to feel safe at a show again. I wanted to get on him and not feel on the edge of a coronary.

I spent last night cleaning, polishing and preparing all my things, washing my favourite numnah and making sure everything was sparkling, mainly to keep myself busy and not fret!

I was surprised to have only made one nervous toilet visit whilst learning my tests and only one more this morning when reality kicked in.

First job...I gave him a calmer syringe! I'm now doubting myself if these are for his benefit or mine, but nevertheless, I'm sticking with it for now!

I got him all plaited and loaded and we arrived with plenty of time to spare in the glorious spring sunshine.

I think the last time I went to a show was New Year's Eve, so you can imagine how full of dread I was about getting on. He just lights up when we go out and I'm scared. I'm scared of his tense upright neck, his bulging eye, seeing his heart pound in his chest, I HATE it. It makes me scared to get on. Today I chatted to Auntie Smurph about this seasons' show attire and took my mind off things.

Surprisingly, Pat was super chilled. No fidgets, no eye bulging, nothing! I got on, no humpy back, no serpent head moments, not a squeak I worked him in outside, away from other horses and then took him indoors to a warm up ring with 5/6 other people riding... BLOODY NOTHING! He was AMAZING!

Into the tests and my word, he was a Dolly Daydream. In fact, it was a far cry from what we are capable of at this level because he was SO chilled! He wasn't forward enough at all, but I felt so safe I could have cried with joy. I didn't once grab my strap or feel that tightness in my chest, I did however, sweat buckets trying to get him going forwards!

So, we earned and deserved our 66% and 68% tests (that could easily be 5% more when we are on top form) for a WIN and a third place. And here we are... back in the game.

I have learnt today; that it's not so bad after all and how you really must get on and 'do' to release your fears... Oh and not to give him the calmer after all, maybe just try without it next time?!

Love as always

Vic and Pat xxxxx

~

Sometimes, just getting out there and realising things aren't as terrifying as you thought, is the only way to get over your fears. I think quite often, your fears are actually very ridiculous and usually stem from not being prepared enough. Most of the time, my fears are quite likely to be guilt related too, because I know I could have done more in the run up. This is what I'm learning about life and about myself and I'm learning it all through the power of equestrianism. They teach you so much about yourself these horses. And with that the call from Bender's trial mum came in…

She loved him, she saw his potential, but she wasn't in a position to offer me money for him. I was so glad that she loved him, and that he had been going so well, that I didn't care about the money by then. It's not like I'm rich but it would also cost me a lot more emotionally to argue the toss. The lady had taken him hacking, jumped him, taken him to 2 dressage shows where he scored nearly 70% in each prelim and he sounded so happy. He wasn't the straightest horse or the most level, but he was happy and doing a good job, so I know it was the right thing for him.

Sometimes, you need to know when to pull that plaster off. **LESSON 4: DON'T HOLD ON FOR TOO LONG**. It might just break you. Whether that's horses, relationships, jobs, cars, houses, packets of bulgar wheat that you've carried around through every house move for ten years… Get rid of the sh*t that isn't making you happy, the stuff that lingers on your conscience and keeps you awake at night. I mean, do you best to fix it if you think there's hope but when you know deep down that all hope is lost. **GIVE UP and MOVE ON.**

You have not failed in giving up, you are in fact stronger and more powerful than ever. Making decisions for your own good is empowering, and the bravest decisions you will ever make. Take it from me.

## APRIL 2018

**Dreams really do come true…**

The start of April was a total wash out. This led to the cancellation of my 'pre-event' due to waterlogging. They had done all they could, but it was terribly wet and there was more rain forecast in the days leading up to it. April showers huh! So, I decided to box up and head to Willow Banks for some jumping instead.

**April 1st 2018**

I'm alive!

So, tonight after yesterday's entry, Auntie Smurph and I took both boys (Pat and Jack) to Willow Banks for the unaffiliated show jumping. I had entered us both for the 80 and the 90cm classes.

Now, we have only been friends for 8 months but, in that time Smurph and I have got to know each other very well. She placates my nerves with funny chatter and I push her out of her comfort zone and swear at her often in return. I think my nerves were in full swing by 2pm because out came a bottle of baileys left over from Christmas to soothe my trembling body!

Yet again I got to the yard and administered the calmer and soon we were ready for the off!

We walked the course, it looked very friendly for my out of practice brain to remember. I tacked up speedily and got on before: 1. It got busier and 2. I cried or followed through!

He warmed up a little sharper than Sunday's dressage but not scary sharp, just manageable and we popped a few warm up jumps! I felt okay, in fact I'd go as far to say that I felt like I was doing it okay. I wasn't hurling him at jumps or tensing last minute, I was just sitting and waiting, sitting and waiting until the jump arrived. Alien to me but I'm getting there! I like to faff you see and this is where it all goes wrong.

So, with no faffing, we went in. The buzzer went, and I got in my rhythm. The first fence jumped awkwardly as the sun was beaming on it, but he did everything I asked, when I asked. He got a bit forward from 3 to 4 but nothing a tickle on the reins didn't fix.

We came out beaming for a super clear round!

Auntie Smurph was next up and felt a bit lacking in zoom but jumped everything clear with a very unfortunate 4 faults for an impromptu circle!

We didn't really gun it round but, in a big class my nippy little lamb came 3rd with 2 ponies pipping him to the red!

Next was Smurph's first ever round at 90cms and I tell you what fellas... she rode for her life!! She was amazing and had just a couple of unlucky rubs, but I was so proud of them!

Pat was in straight after them and he bloody soared the first 6 jumps, he was very careful and gave each one a good bit of room. Then the jump off. The timer started ticking from just before number 7 so I bloody went for it!

I'm no showjumper and my lines and turns were none of finesse, but we flew round for ANOTHER CHUFFING CLEAR!

I cannot tell you how magnificent he felt tonight, like we've picked up where we left off last season and it's all still there, ingrained and happy!

So, waiting on the scores in another huge class... I just got pipped to first place right at the very last rider! But who gives a fat rats ass? NOT ME!

What a bloody horse! He's not jumped much of late and he just came out there like a frigging legend! WE WERE IN THE FRILLIES AGAIN! 2nd place and £20 prize money too.

Gold stars all round.

HUGE love and appreciation for my wonderful horse, he is without doubt or hesitation, the most wonderful soul and I couldn't love him more if I tried.

You know those times where you are just so happy and filled up to the brim with love that you feel like your heart is going to burst open... It might seem daft to most people but, I adore my horse so much, I don't care if we don't jump the biggest jumps or get the best marks for our medium trot, I wouldn't give two hairy balls if I never did another show ever again.

I love his big dark eyes, the little white fluffy fluffle on his lip. I love how from a distance his star makes him look like a Cyclopes. I adore the sound he makes for his food bowl and how he lips up a whole carrot like your posting it in a slot! He makes my heart burst the way he's so timid yet would follow me through the gates of hell if I asked him to.

He is mine, mine to respect, mine to cherish and mine to love for ever.

Love as always

Vic and Pat

Xxxxx

~

I'd been having lessons you see. For the first time in a long time I was have monthly jumping lessons to try and help me work out how to stand more chance of going clear in the phase that I find the hardest. The lady that has been giving me lessons is so good, she understands my nerves and pushes me just far enough out of my comfort zone to get the best out of us both. And isn't that the best feeling, achieving something you didn't think you could.

I was absolutely delighted with our show jumping improvements and that wasn't even the best part of this first week of April. I realise what I am about to write might make you sick to your stomach if all you have ever dreamed of is your own horse transport. I had, and I was about to realise how much that actually meant.

A few days before my 32nd birthday on Easter bank holiday weekend, we made a 7.5hour round trip to meet the loveliest family and bring home the best birthday present I could have ever wished for!

A little blue horse van, a Renault Master built in 1994, with exceptionally low mileage (70k) and a lovely interior with sliding storage and a good solid body with barely a sniff of rust. I had been hiring lorries or sharing lifts for the last 10 years and finally, finally I had my OWN van.

I drove him back 170 miles from Essex to Lincolnshire singing along to his radio at the top of my lungs! And for 3 days afterwards I had to keep going outside and checking that it wasn't all a dream! Huge love and thanks go to my irreplaceable Carrot, for the best birthday present in the world. If there were a 'best husband EVER' contest, he'd be right up there. Dreams really do come true, and I was now free, independent and able to go out whenever the mood took us. And with my first event only a week away, this was almost certainly the start of something great!

**5th April 2018**

Today is Thursday 5th April 2018, it is also exactly 32 years since I arrived into the world.

In 32 years, I have been to 2 schools, 2 universities, lived in over 10 houses, owned 16 animals, ridden over 500 different horses, I have drunk more than my body weight in New Zealand

Sauvignon Blanc and fallen in love at least twice. I have seen death and birth, I have saved lives, I have loved and laughed so much I can't really remember ever being sad.

So today, I am taking this moment to sit back and realise how lucky I am to be alive, to be healthy and happy. To have good friends, family and love surrounding my life. To appreciate myself and how I have grown into the person I am right now.

It is SO important to love yourself for who you are, don't try to be more like anyone but you. You are unique, you are the only one like you, so make sure you realise just how extraordinary you can be. Don't compare, don't look back with regret, be proud of who you are and feel excited about what you are going to bring to the world.

Thank you so very much for your endless support and love, you are part of me and who I am now, and without being able to raise up other people, I know I wouldn't be so happy in myself.

I would love it if you could do me a MEGA favour today, please go and look in the mirror, look at your scraggly un-brushed hair and tell yourself 'I LOVE ME for ME!' and then tell one other person in your life how much you love them too.

Mend the silly arguments, build people up who feel sad and don't let anyone tell you you're not good enough, you are, because I said so.

Lots of love on this special day

Vic xxx

~

Another few days of heavy downpours led to another cancelled event. Nothing was running up and down the country. The whole of April and now most of May were written off for us in Affiliated competitions. Last season I had already done 4 events by the time this season has any chance of getting off the ground. I can't say that I felt that relieved either, I pay an annual fee to be a member of British Eventing, this was going to waste and I couldn't see me fitting more events in later on to compensate.

2018, the year of the non-starter! And yes, I started to get a bit flat and restless. Just as I got my little van, I had no-where to go! I turned my attention to an unaffiliated run at the end of April and booked a jumping lesson and a group pole work session to give me something to keep us on track.

I did, however find it very hard to pull my finger out and get motivated with all this rain. If I have learnt anything about myself lately it is; even though eventing puts the fear of God into me, I wouldn't be the same without it.

I was about to foolishly change my goal posts, easy enough when your armchair eventing! I didn't just want to feel confident jumping 80cms... I wanted to do the very best I could at being confident full stop.

I felt so determined, I had fire in my belly and I wanted to feel good again. I had felt off games because there were no games, and a bit lack lustre and down in the dumps. This can make you lazy, flat and not going anywhere. I vowed to change this starting 'tomorrow'.

**LESSON NUMBER FIVE: TOMORROW NEVER COMES.** If you wait until tomorrow to change things, you will always be the same. It's true, tomorrow NEVER arrives because when it is tomorrow, the next day will then be tomorrow… it really never comes!

Why are you putting it off? What's stopping you changing things RIGHT NOW? Changing your mind set in that moment will be enough, you can action the changes in the future, but change things NOW or don't bloody bother. Remain mediocre for the rest of your existence, see if I care…! But you have SO much potential to be so much more, why wouldn't you take that chance?

I hope you can see how much potential you have to achieve greatness. I want to help you to work out how to get somewhere you want to be.

Whether you feel unfulfilled at work, you want to be a better rider or win more rosettes. If you want to be a better wife or mother, go after something you have been too afraid of or try something you have never done before... you CAN do those things.

It might seem a million miles away right now but taking those first steps makes you at least half a million miles closer than someone not willing to try.

What is it that you want to do? What puts a fire in your belly? What gets you out of bed in a morning?

I'm not advising you all go out and quit your jobs today, but I am advising that you to never, ever settle for a mediocre life. We get one go at this life, just one. Make sure you haven't left the world with things you wished you'd done or wished you'd tried harder for.

Today, let's make a change, make a difference and be the brilliant people that we all could be with just a few small changes. Don't feel disheartened if your dreams are something no one else has succeeded at. Pave a way, following will only get you to the same place as someone else. Don't fear being different, because you are so unique, there is already no-one like you!

YOU have so much POWER and so much skill you might not even know about yet....

~

The week leading up to my first (unaffiliated) event of the season I felt so prepared. I had learnt and practiced my test quite far in advance, packed up MY lorry and, because of this, my nerves were almost under control. I was desperate to get out there and see what happened without any expectations, and also see how much we had forgotten since October. So here it is… NUMBER 1:

**EPWORTH 80cms Unaffiliated Event**

I awoke that morning to a terrible bout of nerves, a VERY unsettled tummy and the fear I had been waiting for... I was back to square one all over again. I felt a failure before arrival, how was I ever going to claw that back?!

I dragged my beloved in from the field and got him ready for our departure time of 12pm for a dressage of 13.50. Plaited, brushed and ready to go, we set off and arrived in plenty of time without soiling myself and without any fuss. Can I just say, how proud and lucky I felt turning up in my OWN lorry? I've never felt so appreciative of anything in my whole life, it's my independence and I am so grateful to finally have my own wheels.

Having yet to walk the course, I collected my number and visited the porta-loo before tacking up ready for dressage. It was a little walk down to the warm up, but this was a great thing, it meant I could settle him in a little bit without the company of too many others. Only a few salmon fish moments and he settled okay. I'd have liked another ten minutes, but we were called down to our arena quite speedily!

In the ring, I did my best with what I had on the day. He was still sharp and still threatened the snake head moves he knows I hate... we made it through with no balls ups and came out smiling but guessing at around a 33 score.

*NOTE: In eventing dressage, the lowest score is the best. The test is marked as a percentage like normal, with a mark for each movement and then reversed to give you a point score.*

*Hopefully this is in the twenties, usually it's in the 30's but sometimes disappointingly in the 40s.*

Anyway, a two-hour gap until my show jumping meant a course walk for both courses. Now, I'm not that keen on walking the cross-country course on the day as I'm usually knackered from the riding bit, but today I felt ok and there was nothing too hideous on the course! Well, there was number 7 and 8, and I didn't like the water much... but 1-4 looked doable at least!

Back at the box, we dressed for show jumping and got mounted. I felt stupidly nervous now. I don't even know exactly why, we've done more show jumping lately than anything else, so I should feel okay, but the course wasn't riding very well and there were a lot of fillers.

Warmed up and ready to go in, I discreetly showed him a couple of fillers before the bell, he was not accepting of them. The round that ensued was an absolute bloody shambles.

He spooked, jinked, looked and generally made hard work of what should have been a breeze. I nearly came off between 5 and 6, lost my stirrup and flapped about around his neck for a minute... but I stayed on, the poles stayed up (to my absolute amazement) and we soared the last for a bloody clear round!

Now, at this point we knew our dressage was joint leader in the section, which meant going XC in contention of the win. This is the absolute WORST THING you can tell me before the off!

Dressed and down in the cross country warm up, it was now or never. I had to put out of my mind, all of the doubts and worries of not having jumped a solid fence since Norton Disney last season. I gunned round the warm up jumping not just the 80 ones but, the bigger ones too and it felt bloody amazing. Pat hadn't forgotten, and I wasn't a wobbling, crying sack of sh*t. I quickly went down to the start box before doubt had a chance to creep in.

Those famous last words of the cross country starter; "3....2...1.....Have a good ride!"

The first fence, a wooden barrel arrangement, came up far quicker than I had anticipated, I rode for it like it was about to set alight, we were ON FIRE!! Galloping to the second, a wooden house; he backed off but boy I wasn't letting anything slip just yet... I fired him at it and he soared in reply. The third; a chicken coop, obviously had brutally murdered chickens still screaming inside it.... he backed off so much we nearly ground to a stop. I seriously had to give it some welly, but he answered my arse kicking and flew it in the end.

A gallop down to a white arrow head at 4, which jumped much better than I thought it would (and much better than 3!!), down to a hay wagon at 5 clad with spooky bales! He backed right off again despite my encouragement... I thought, this is where we come unstuck. But bugger me! He jumped it from nearly a stand still!

6 was a set of rails that I gunned it for and got a confident and bold jump (at last!) 7a was a roll top, up a bank to 7b, a log pile and drop... I slowed up to trot for this b element. I'm glad I did because it was new for us and rather unseating.

8 was in the trees and actually jumped very nicely for a long gallop down to 9; a castle. I yipped, and he soared this. He was absolutely flying now and felt just like where we left off last year. I screamed with joy down to 10 and 11, so happy that we got our rhythm back, our hearts beating as one around this bold course.

Back to reality, 12 and 13 were very kind, solid and wide but not spooky and then 14; the water, straight in and out no bother! 15; a double of flower dressed pipes, he looked but I yipped and squealed, and he flew them on a lovely stride! Galloping down to the big carrot box to finish, we got a fantastic shot at the last and screamed through the finish line absolutely bloody delighted!

I cannot tell you what today felt like and what it meant to me. I thought our time was up in this sport, I thought my nerves couldn't take another season, but today I proved I can do it. I can be brave, I can ride like my life depends on it. I can, and I did. I gave everything I had today, and we finished up on 32.8, 2.8 time penalties (too fast!) to add to our dressage of 30.0, DOUBLE CLEAR!

We were laying in first place for a very long time, but those 2.8tf were expensive. First place was out of sight, but we weren't out of the prizes. We finished in 4th with a lovely numnah, fly spray and rosette as winnings!

I cannot tell you what it means to have this Wimpy outlet for my documentary, it really keeps me going. The support and wishes of good luck, knowing that there are so many people willing us round that course is the reason I ride for my life. Thank you with all the energy I have left.

What a day, what a bloody lion-hearted horse and what a way to start our season.

Huge, huge thanks to Auntie Smurph for grooming, to Daddy Carrot as chief photographer and to my sponsors for supporting us so kindly, and generously this year. Without them, and without you, I'd be nowhere near the rider I am.

Thank you

Love as always

Vic and Pat xxxxx

~

## May 2018

## A New Perspective

As regular as a pendulum on a grandfather clock, my elation over that first event didn't last for ever and anxiety started creeping back in. It's a funny thing; emotion. I often wonder if I am ever-so slightly bi-polar because I never really have long periods of just 'being'. I have the busiest brain of anyone I know, and I'm never really satisfied with things, just the way they are. I spend so much time striving for something better, something more or something different, I forget to just breathe and enjoy the right now. That definitely comes at a cost. I get exhausted easily, and the bad days feel all-consuming while the good days get less often.

**7th May 2018**

Anxiety, a constant battle with that uncertain feeling.

Monday morning, 5.45am.

I'm awake over an hour before the alarm again but not because I can't wait to bounce out of bed and start an exciting day. But because I'm riddled with this sinking emotion.

It's not sadness exactly, I can hear birds singing, I'm not sad. It's not grief either, I haven't lost anything, or have I? It's worry, fear, guilt, self-loathing, and feeling lost in myself and it eats me away inside.

I'm going through a period of change in my working life. My security blanket of my main income (30 hours a week) is being pulled from under me and I'm panicking. This is not a surprise, this was agreed months ago but I'm still not ready! I set up a business to attract new clients before this event, but because I was so desperately lacking in confidence when I did it, I haven't felt right pushing it or in fact charging people for my time!

Yesterday I slept, almost 16 hours out of 24. I wanted to not think about anything. I wanted to feel nothing; no stress, no doubt, no panic. Instead I prolonged the inevitable.

It's the most debilitating feeling, not feeling good enough. I don't feel attractive, I'd go as far to say that I quite dislike myself. I don't feel as though my husband wants to be with me anymore, why would he? When I have nothing to offer.

Now, here's the thing, I am absolutely not looking for sympathy, I'm making it very clear that despite what an Instagram feed or Facebook page portray, behind it could be a broken mirror. People going through things that you couldn't even see until the cracks appear.

And on reasoning with myself, I think that it's okay to feel this way. It's okay to feel out of your depth and struggling to keep your head out of water long enough to take a breath. It's okay to hate yourself, to feel as though you don't belong. Because, **LESSON NUMBER 6: THIS. IS. NOT. PERMANENT!**

And I know this, because I've felt this way before. I made changes, got my sh*t together and fought for a life I deserve.

I won't let this beat me; not now, not ever. I'm off to learn to love myself, to feel proud again and be the best version of me that I can.

Don't feel alone, you're not. I'm here.

Love as always

Vic

Xxxx

~

I find a lot of this hard to read, just like you. But I bet your life you've felt it too. That feeling where just feel gross. Do you know what snaps me out of it the quickest? Giving some time to myself.

I'm a very happy person in general and I would literally walk over hot coals if you told me it would make you feel better, but I do have quite low self-esteem and regularly feel a bit of an underdog in a lot of areas in my life.

I find that giving myself an easy few hours, putting on some makeup, riding my horse and then enjoy drinking wine with my husband after work makes everything instantly much better.

Why on earth wouldn't you take full advantage of being alive, of having choices, of having the freedom to live.

Don't you dare let one day go by where you don't feel good enough, there might be no tomorrow.

Don't spend time planning in and preparing when you have no real intention of doing either.

Don't wait for things to come to you, make something for yourself.

Don't wait for life to happen, make it your own, take hold of it by the reins and go out and get what you deserve.

Make yours happy and don't wait... you are brilliant, just look deeper.

I think it's very important to look after ourselves mentally. Think about you, about how you woke up feeling. Talking about things and airing them out instead of trying to pretend it's all ok is what I'm getting at.

Waking up worried is not nice, particularly for weeks at a time

I often feel like I have a lot on my plate, like work is getting left because of the books, I worry that this book isn't as I want it yet, the horses haven't been ridden since Friday and I'm worried about getting back on, THE LIST GOES ON!! I'm falling apart a bit at the seams with my sciatica which isn't helping. And Carrot and I haven't "done it" in ages and I'm worried I'm a crap wife! I worry about getting fat, I worry about people at work thinking I'm sh*t, I'm worried that I haven't got children yet, etc. I just fret all the time. But do you know something else, THIS IS ALSO NORMAL!!!!

It's VERY likely that a lot of you worry about worrying too, but what does it achieve? If there is nothing you can do right that second, why fret about it. You don't get anywhere on a rocking horse, and that's what worry is.

Just breathe. Take a step back, make a list of the things you have to deal with and turn them all into positives, and you'll soon realise how little you can affect each one...

Are you alive?

Are you looking forward to anything?

Are you going to grab whatever good comes your way and make the best of today?

The thing is, you might not see it right now, but you are just like me, we are all brilliant for something and sometimes we are worried about showing how brilliant we really are. Well b*llocks!! I'm going to be exactly that today, join me will you!!

Be the best you today, ride like it's your last ride, make a nice dinner, eat a cream cake, hug a friend, tell someone you love them, just make sure when you are in bed tonight that you can look back and smile.

I want you to see how special and brilliant you are.

Love yourself before anything else because it isn't just something that will affect my riding, it will affect your work, your relationships and most importantly, your health.

So, what is it that we need to do?

Essentially, we need to work at being proud, not feeling ashamed to blow your own trumpet and not entertain that downward spiral of self-deprecating thoughts.

**Day one is right now... Do something for me will you. Write down 3 things that make you proud of yourself – RIGHT HERE. Physically write them down and put them somewhere you can see them at least three times a day.**

**And start believing them.**

***Thing Number 1.***

***Thing Number 2.***

***Thing Number 3.***

Try it, I don't think I know anyone that ever gives themselves enough credit... bloody well love YOU a bit more.

With this self-loving in mind, I wanted to throw myself into a new challenge. One that was massively rewarding, if a little outside of my comfort zone. I made a deal with Auntie Smurph last year, that if she jumped the big rails out on our ride, I would start teaching again. She bloody jumped them, didn't she!! So, here I was fulfilling my side of the deal and agreeing to teach at a Nervous and Novice Confidence Day Camp for the local Riding Club!

**17th May 2018**

2 months ago I got a text from my dear friend Liz, asking if I fancied helping her out with a bit of "motivational instructing" at a Nervous and Novice camp in May... it seemed such a long way off, and I'm at the stage in life where I will literally do ANYTHING to help anyone, so I agreed!

The day came, Liz sent me my agenda with my groups (plural) that I would be allocated, and it turns out I was set to impart wisdom upon 4 groups of 5 riders over the course of the day.

I think I fretted just as much as I would before an event! It's been a long time, almost 10 years, since I was actively teaching people to feel less crap, less scared, and more empowered on their horses.

I work very much on the basis of what I would need to hear, and my lovely groups were all made up of riders that lack confidence and self-belief, not necessarily ability, just like me. The only thing I cared about was that I wanted them to leave my arena more confident about themselves than when they came in.

"Today, I don't give a sh*t about outline, engagement or learning half pass...!" I think I said this a lot! But all I cared about was their confidence, happiness, self-worth. This will *make* you as a rider long before getting your horses head down will.

My first group were lovely. I was a little nervous, but I just put myself in their shoes and realised I was the one to be afraid of! I bellowed at them, cheered them on and made them all gallop down the long side of the arena until they smiled the whole length! We played pony games and spent some time without stirrups. I explained how to drop from the hip, how to relax on a horse and learning to feel tension and how to roll it away.

I repeated this format for the next groups, they were responsive, they all tried really hard and one lady in particular who came in very upset after being bronched with whilst getting on, did so well. I felt so desperately proud seeing her in a forward seat cantering down the school!

At the end, I pulled them in and thanked them all. I confess to tearing up rather unprofessionally, but I was full to the brim with pride for what these ladies achieved. Tears of pride are the very best ones.

I am so glad I pushed myself out of my comfort zone to do this, it was a brilliant day and I couldn't have wished for a kinder and lovelier bunch of people to dust myself off in front of.

Thank you to Liz, who always has such kind things to say about me, she is such a lovely person and a very, very good teacher herself. Thank you to my husband too, who took me through my lessons the night before over a gin and tolerated my nerves yet again!

~

With my arse in gear, I decided to take inspiration from these ladies I taught and knuckle down in preparation for my next event in a weeks' time. Pat is always better at an event if I have managed to get him out somewhere in the days leading up to it. So that's what I did. Carrot, Pat and I hopped into the Wimpy Wagon and popped down to Hill House, our lovely, local venue. I busted out 2 Novice tests taking 2$^{nd}$ and 3$^{rd}$ place in a tight class. I was so happy to be out on a balmy evening with my boys, I didn't really care what the outcome was as long as it was non-death.

This led nicely into the first affiliated event of the season. A BE90 at Shelford, a venue I was familiar with after two of my events last season being held there. Should have put my mind at rest right?!

**EVENT NUMBER 2: Shelford BE90**

So, my routine outing before the big day was complete with my dressage trip on Friday night, I gave him a little pop over some jumps in the field yesterday to round off our prep. I then went to my big brothers for a family barbecue, drank a bottle of wine to myself and got a crap night's sleep... brilliantly done you whopping sack of cr*p. Why did I do that? Why? Maybe to dull the nerves, maybe that's it? Either way, I was an idiot!

But anyway, I woke up feeling like a turtle had deposited its innards into my skull and had no one to blame but myself!

My first AFFLIATED 90 of the season, only my second run out this year too. I was dressaging at 12.30pm with a two-hour gap before jumping at 3pm, so I left the course walk until then and luckily didn't have to rush. We arrived in plenty of time and I began flushing my system with litres of water and went and checked in. I was nearly last to go in the section and there were already some very competitive scores written down on the board.

Back at the box, I got tacked up and headed for the warm-up. He worked in really well with not too many moments where I felt scared this time. I'd given him the calmer syringe before we left home, so it was in full flow in time for my most dreaded part (the dressage warm up). I came out quite optimistic for a sub 30 but alas, a 33 was what we received. Bizarrely this is the 3rd time I've been to Shelford and each time his scores have been 3 – 4 marks worse than anywhere else. I haven't seen my sheet yet to learn how to improve, I guess he was a bit behind the leg at times, but

I've done much worse tests for better marks so it's all a learning game.

*NOTE: Behind the leg – is where, no matter how much you think you're travelling forwards, it's not enough. If you took the frantically kicking leg away, would the horse stop? If yes, he is almost certainly 'behind the leg'.*

We were lying around 8th going into the show jumping though so I'll take that.

The cross country course walk was not ideal, not a disaster by any stretch, but definitely not ideal. There were a few I didn't like; the skinny house at 4, the feed bags in front of number 9 and the size of the hedge at 13… but aside from that, it wasn't horrendous.

Into the show jumping warm up and the calmer had almost definitely worn off, Pat was salmon fishing, squeaking and ballooning after every jump. I was not having a nice time AT ALL. He was thoroughly enjoying himself whilst my white knuckles clung on for grim death. He felt strong but not in a confident way, more in a 'leg it back to the lorry' kind of way, and this was not funny.

In the ring, I felt totally out of my comfort zone, normally my quite easy to manoeuvre horse felt like steering a double decker bus through soft butter. He was strong, and I didn't like it. The jumps felt small, there was nothing to back him off and I'll admit it; I needed a bigger fence today. I never thought I'd say that, but he was running on and I was not enjoying it! But despite his exuberance, we just rolled one rail where I over checked and only had 4 to add to our dressage score!

Now, I will just add that this time last year I would have been thrilled with that, but I've been working so hard to ride him better, I can't help but pick holes. I left him too slow, I needed more power, it was totally my error and I will fix it! MUST enjoy going fast.

A quick change of clothes and we were turning a very lovely shade of green walking to the XC warm up. I don't think I've been this nervous for a long time. I walked for a good 20 minutes before the chest tightness subsided, I stopped blubbering and I got my sh*t together!! We sailed a few practice jumps and went into the Start box of Doom....

It really is now or never when you hear that "you've got 30 seconds" call out. What the f*ck can you do about it then...? NOTHING absolutely sweet FA, so you may as well give it everything you've got!

3, 2, 1.... we flew out of the start box and galloped down to the first; a log shared with the BE80 course, phew...! A nice easer-inner and it jumped nicely which always gives me extra beans. A short gallop to the second, which was a wooden upright shared with the BE100... excellent! But I gave it some power and shouted "GO GOOOOO GOOOOOOOOO...." and go he did! Soaring over it with room to spare, and onto number 3.

Three hadn't looked much when I walked it, but he bloody backed off it a treat (wasurk!) so I had to ride for my life here, long before I had anticipated. It wasn't pretty...but we got over it! Down to the skinny house at 4, I shortened the canter and rode through the invisible funnel with nice short reins and a firm leg, and he pinged out over it like a bloody pro!

A gallop down to 5; a trailer dressed with two (obviously, life threatening) wooden acorns. He looked, looked again, thought about stopping but I caught him, picked him up and carried him over with a lot of vocal encouragement. I'm so used to his backing off now, I know if I want it enough, he goes! Into the woods for a palisade at six and a set of ladders at seven, both jumped really nicely after the killer acorns.

8 was a double of plastic pipes and he was so busy spooking at the jump judge we almost didn't lock on, but we got there, Pop! Pop! By now I have a few things running through my head;

- Ecstatic delirium
- Holding back the tears of joy
- How likely is it that a human being can cough up an actual lung?

If I have learnt anything from today, it's that I'm not fit enough for this part, that's for sure!

9 was the bags of feed... he backed off, but I was seriously ready for him and kicked his arse so royally over those bags that he galloped like the clappers over a log and drop for 10a and b into the trees. I grabbed a lot of mane down the bank and good job because 11; a log out of the woods, left me a little unseated, but he really did help me out there!

12 was a step up which was no bother for his Nibs, then a gallop down to the whopping hedge at 13, probably the best jump I got all day. It felt amazing... soaring through the air, squealing with joy! 14 was on an angle back into the woods again and was catching a lot of people out, I pulled back to a strong trot just for the turn and cantered the last few strides.. ping! We nailed it! Out over the palisade at 15 and a nice gallop down to another hedge before the water!

In we splashed and out over the yellow pipes, soaring and squealing down the home straight to fly over the last and through those wonderful finish flags....

Huge pats and squeals all round! Pat came bucking and leaping, full of beans through the finish. He genuinely felt the happiness

I felt. He was having the time of his life today, I could just feel it bursting out of him!

The love I have for that tiny boy, I don't care that he's not the bravest or the most careful or that we haven't won one yet. All I care about is how we gel together, how we are a team. We know each other inside out and that's worth more than any rosette could ever be.

So that was it, inside the optimum time too for a finishing score of 37 leaving us in 11th place. Not bad at all for our first affiliated run and lots to take from it too. I'm happy, he's happy, that's what it all boils down to.

Thank you to my Carrot for being the best groom and chief photographer and for his never ending support.

Also, a big thank you to everyone that came and said hello today. You guys are the reason I'm doing this, you keep me going and you've built up my fragile confidence and given me hope. So, thank you with everything I have left.

Good night, God bless and so much love, as always

Vic and Pat

Xxxxxxx

~

I was so pleased to have got back out at an affiliated event and not to have ballsed it up too much. Eventing takes all kinds of emotion; the preparation, planning, fitness, the stuff you have to buy just to even get there. It's not easy, it's hard work and you have to enjoy it otherwise it's an awful lot of heartache. The feeling I get afterwards is the best feeling ever, that invincibility that lasts for days. I expect the top riders feel it too, only on a much higher scale! We are a rare breed us 'Horse People' and deep down we are all the same. I want to share with you a few of the things that unite us and bring us together, the reasons I love being part of this madness;

First up…There is no other sport in the world that sees even the tiniest human masterfully control what was once a wild animal, and guide it through a dance routine, through flags and over death defying obstacles with total finesse. Those tiny racing jockeys who go so fast on these cherished beasts that they have to wear goggles so that their eyeballs don't fly out – you, my friends, are like no-one on earth, you are GOD. Number one, has to be a love for a sport like no other.

Number two - It doesn't matter whether you are 92 or 12, being 'pony mad' and having a phone cover with your beloved horse on it, is perfectly acceptable at any age. You can re-live your youth well into those twilight years and no-one will think you have early onset Alzheimer's. This includes clicking your tongue to get someone to move rather than saying 'excuse me please!'. Reason 2; being marginally insane but in very good company.

Number three - The overall appearance. Being on public transport, in a supermarket, at the dentist, in the office, etc. post-yard/pre-shower and mouthing to the cashier; 'Sorry, I've come straight from RIDING MY HORSE!' is deemed acceptable in our circles. Wearing odd and often brightly coloured socks over too tight (sometimes stained) breeches and carrying foliage around in our un-brushed hair is certainly not a problem for us, we see it as time saving, making us PERFECT marriage material! Reason 3; WE ARE UNIQUE and marching to the beat of our own drum!

Number four - The etiquette. Where else will you learn that a.) Your needs/feelings will NEVER come first. Stop thinking they will, your horses' needs come first! b.) That you should always pass wide and slow and drive with caution, making you the perfect road user! c.) That when pushing a supermarket trolley, regardless of cucumber location, you pass left hand to left hand.

So many other things 'non-equestrians' are missing out on... Reason 4; you can guarantee we've been dragged up in terrific style.

Essentially, being an equestrian affiliates you to a not-so-secret club, one that you will always be a part of whether you own a horse or not; 'For the Love of the Horse Club'. We are all united, we all shared something in common, we all LOVE horses.

We must stop tearing strips off one another, we have all smelt of p*ss, have had hay in our hair and have tasted a mouthful of soil after a fall. We all have the ability to put our beautiful horses before ourselves so there is absolutely no reason why we shouldn't support a fellow horse lover for doing the same.

You should feel proud to be an equestrian, I do.

## June 2018

## The Highs and Lows of Eventing

**3rd June 2018**

So, a last minute entry into the 90cms Show-cross at Epworth Equestrian Ltd saw us power trotting around our regular hacking route last night in an attempt to tire out my keener that usual pony ready for the big day. Normally I like to get out somewhere but with time being tight, a decent hack would have to do.

*NOTE: Show-Cross is like eventing, only cheaper and with no dressage – just show jumping and cross country elements.*

Now, Pat was super forward at Shelford last week. He was jumping out of his skin and it frightened me a little bit. I wanted him to be a bit sluggish, so I could manoeuvre him around a bit more with confidence before our next BE at Speetley on the 10th.

We walked the course that afternoon and whilst it was super big and bold with a lot of fences shared with the 100, I didn't feel too frightened and was ready to take the challenge on. After a good sweaty hack, I gave him a lovely bath, loaded the lorry and felt very ready for our event today. For once, I felt ready. Yes, nervous. Yes, plagued with loose bowels and frequent toilet visits, but I was ready.

My times were 2.16pm and straight out on the XC at 2.45pm

Carrot and I loaded up at 12pm ready to arrive in lots of time to hopefully catch Auntie Smurph storm her first clear cross country, but alas, it was not to be.

The sound of my lorry was not how I left it. Carrot "borrowed" the Wimpy Wagon to pick up a new motorbike one evening last week and thought it sensible not to tell me that the speedo had stuck and that the noises coming from his under-carriage were not normal. He wouldn't have known but, there was an upset tummy in there somewhere.

I didn't push him, just drove him at my usual Sunday driver speed and 10 minutes away from home, I lost all power. In fact, not just power, it became apparent that Wimpy's innards had spilled out underneath his sexual body and were scraping along the tarmac.

F******************CK!!!

PANIC set in, I indicated and luckily pulled in at a local dairy farm just off the main road. My heart was in shreds, my nerves frayed and with tears stinging my eyes we phoned roadside assistance. My beloved Wimpy Wagon parked up with his innards on show for all to see. And in 25 degrees, my sweating pony was on the back.

This is where karma repays you dividends. My lovely friend Kate and her Mum were driving to the same show and were 2 minutes from us. They stopped in and even though fate was trying to delay my run today, I unloaded my boy and hopped him up onto Kate's lovely lorry along with my essentials leaving Carrot at the Wimpy Wagon waiting for the recovery.

On arrival, I felt ridiculously out of sorts. I was dribbling about, disorganised and with no grasp on time, found myself flapping about at the last minute. Not great! I warmed up and normally, the calmer syringe distributed on departure ready for the sharpness in the dressage warmup was almost certainly a mistake. He felt flat, lumpy and not very forward. I didn't feel scared though, which is a silver lining of course.

I've never had a smooth show jumping round at Epworth, they have a lot to look at in the way of fillers and banners, and Pat is always a spooky little sh*t there. Today was NO different.

We went in, I got my canter WAY too late and managed to scrape over the first 3 fine, I turned left to the double at 4, put my leg on as he backed off (standard) and the little b*stard slammed the anchors on for the second part of a one stride double. This hasn't happened in 6 years... he's never just said no. But I watched the video back; I was up his neck, not really in a position of determination and I deserved it. It has definitely taught me to sit the hell up after a fence.

I circled and represented for him to try again, he jumped the first part and went to drop the anchors again, but this time I was cross. I rode that jump and the rest of the course like it was the last thing I was ever going to do. Determined, leg on, no second chances and we got round with a score of 12.

By Jove, I was exhausted and not feeling overly confident going cross country after that.

I put my medical arm band on, offered Captain Spookerson a drink and off we went to warm up for the death phase.

I jumped a couple of practice fences and went straight through to the start. I hadn't studded up for this and what a massive mistake. He skidded a little into the first fence, looking at it like a turd. He jumped it, but it felt horrid. The second wasn't much better; a roll top, he looked and thought about backing off but I nailed his arse and we scraped over.

Round a right hand bend to 3; a hedge and 4; the upturned boat, both jumped much better than I thought they would. A gallop down to the castle at 5 and he felt heavy, I also felt exceptionally out of breath and tight in the chest. I toyed with pulling up, there was still so much of the course to go, I just didn't feel like I could get around.

I wanted to cry. I felt sh*t.

I don't know quite what made me decide to carry on, but I found something from somewhere and came to the roll top and coffin at 6 and with grit and a good kick, we sailed both and galloped down to the biggest fence on course, a big grey table. I hit a duff stride because of him backing off, again. But he jumped it, just a bit backwards.

Now, I rarely ever smack this horse, but we weren't going to get round safely unless something changed. I thwacked him twice on the bottom and he pricked up down to the wishing well. 3 strides out he clocked the water which was straight after this fence and I screamed at him "help me out lad"... annoyed at being smacked, I obviously didn't deserve his help and he stopped.... STOPPED, DEAD.

I smacked his bottom again. It was stupid, it was my fault, I was massively on the defensive and I asked for his help. No... that's not the way it works! He asks me for help, that's our deal, not the other way around. I deserved that stop 100% and put it right behind me and kicked on, sailing it on the second attempt.

Over the big carrot table and up a bank to fly over some pipes and run back down, all rode fine. Then up over a wooden house to my only worry on the course, a log off a step with 4 strides to a skinny... well, I needn't have worried. I did what I set out to, ignored the log, locked us on to the next fence and we flew them both, no bother.

A gallop down to the wagon one from home and I really chased him in for a good confident finish, he sailed the last and we were home. Finally, home, safe and well.

Now, on paper it was the worst f*cking day I think I've had out competing EVER! My lorry exhaust somewhere on the A15, my Carrot stranded with the van, my disastrous show jumping fails and a stop on the cross country course. But I felt elated with another beefy 90 under our belts. So what, we made some boo boo's, we're alive and well!

Something didn't feel right though, I didn't feel right, I felt weak and lacking in muscular fitness. My brain wasn't engaged, and my stirrups were set 3 holes lower than normal by mistake. I felt like a wet weekend in Bognor Regis and it showed in my results.

Not every day can be brilliant, not every run can be smooth, but it's these testing ones that we learn the most from. I will NEVER ride like that again as long as I live, I will never let him down or smack him for my failings.

Today was a day for learning, AGAIN.

Thank you so much to Kate and her mum for being there to pick us up and for being so kind. To my dear Smurph who stormed around her first 80 like she's been doing it forever (I'm so proud of them) and to my poor Carrot who I'm sure would have loved a hot dog at the show far more than waiting for a recovery man on the road side.

Now I need to get a new exhaust before Saturday and rest my drained body before dusting off and knuckling down in hope of picking up a Regional final ticket!

Thank you all for your endless support as always, sorry to have let you down today.

Love as always

Vic and Pat xxxxx

~

Possibly the cruddiest start to June I could have had but we were both safe and the van could be mended, it would all be fine. I felt really bloody flat about how I rode him on the cross country though and I wished I hadn't smacked him. He was obviously feeling out of sorts too. I didn't have long to get sorted for Speetley and this was a bit of the unknown for me. A venue I had never been to. I was really hoping to get a Regional final ticket for Badminton Grassroots but to do that you need to be in the top 10% of your section and the way things were going, this wasn't look that great!

I spent the week preparing my test and felt confident that I could get a good one bashed out on the day. Even if I was losing a few marks here and there, he was consistently in the low 30's which would just be enough if I could keep all the poles in the cups! To test this theory, I popped down to Willow Banks this week too and bloody nailed two clear rounds. The training is definitely paying off!! But it wasn't long until the day arrived, and with the Wimpy Wagon back on the road (and me £300 lighter), we were set and ready to go!

**EVENT NUMBER 3 : Speetley BE90**

So, Here it is... my 2nd BE event of the season.

As you will have read, I had a total knock in every sense last Sunday at Epworth with a refusal in the show jumping and another out on course... It was a day for learning not to ride like a sack of sh*t but it was also a BIG wake up call to how fragile confidence really is.

I went out and boxed away my show jumping demons at Willow Banks on Wednesday night with TWO clears at 80 and 90cms to put some wind back in our sails for today.

Yesterday evening I ran through our test again and he was so lovely and worked so hard that I slept quite well (after a few cheeky whites in the pub afterwards!)

I wasn't on until 13.36 for dressage and with the venue only 1.5hours away, I didn't have to leave until 11am. Good and bad having afternoon times, as you get all morning to empty your pride into the loo but you also don't have to rush around or wake your husband up too early.

I sent the usual message to Daddy Carrot, who was out for an early fishing trip saying; "I don't think I want to go today..." STANDARD wet fish!

We arrived in good time, stopped on the way for fuel and a McDonalds (YEP... that's right, I actually ATE something for the first time EVER on the morning of an event, 4 and a half "chicken" McNuggets) and once parked up, went and got my number and registered my attendance.

I didn't have much time to fret and got him ready and mounted for my dressage time. He warmed up the BEST he has EVER done. I'm trialling a new bit to attempt to get a bit more consistency in the contact and what a difference this has made in just a few sessions! He's forward and not blocked in front, much more rideable and I thoroughly enjoyed our warm up today. In the arena he spooked at EVERYTHING down one side and I thought there would be a lot of marks reflecting that tension, but alas, with some good marks for the not so tense parts, we managed to score 30, a top 5 score in our section.

Next up, the course walk. Holy Mother of Christmas.... the HEDGE OXER was bloody gigantic!! I mean, seriously large. I think if I had walked the course yesterday, I would have bailed.

The show jumping was also causing problems and had LOADS of fillers. Not great after our recent stoppage experience at all.

I got back on and went down to the warm up, a few things I changed today. Number 1. The bit, Number 2. I put a fly veil on him and 3. I didn't just sit there like a wet fart on a hot day. I jumped 5 or 6 practice jumps and we elected to go in before our time for the first time ever!

In the ring, he was having a good look, but I tried to keep the rhythm, I brought him back to change a canter lead and other than number 7 that he gawped at and got a big kick, he jumped a fantastic CLEAR ROUND! I cried with utter joy when I left the arena, but lucky for me waiting to go in was the nicest young lad Ben, who hugged me (both still on horseback) and sent me on my very merry way.

So, I didn't know my dressage score yet and I didn't want to. We got ready and walked down to the death phase feeling a little green. It was very quiet, in fact there was only me in there warming up and the course didn't have a single rider out on it, so I jumped 2 or 3 warm up jumps and went to the box.

3....2....1.... Out the start box like a bullet we flew, pounding up to the flower box at one. I kept my leg on firm and he sailed over for a confident start. A gallop uphill back towards the lorries and he was giving it great guns until 3 strides out, I snapped out of wet fart mode and smacked him on the bottom. It was a risk, but he replied with a lovely jump over the 2nd; a milk churn under a rail. Around the corner to three; a bloody fruit and veg stand. No-one is in the market for a pound of plums in that situation, I'm sure. He eyeballed it, but I wasn't letting him stop. I got an awful shot at it, but we cleared it. Putting it behind us, we soared down to the next fence.

A gallop to 4; a roll top of sorts. He didn't look at it much because I was driving like Jenson Button on acid. Down to the double at 5; another roll top, which jumped really well on a great forward stride, to a rail with a flower box in the hedge line. He dropped the anchors and we ground to a snail pace, but my heart had sailed over long before then and by some miracle, my body and my horse made it to the other side too! 6 was another open rail with a left turn and gallop to the HEDGE OF DEATH! I kicked like never before, I growled, I shouted obscenities that would have been heard in all neighbouring counties, and we bloody soared like the wind over that big beast!

Down to the water at 8; a jump before the moisture, was very aptly named the 'PUNT' (replace one letter if you will!) that was causing a few problems for others. I brought him back to a more balanced canter and growled like an old fish wife and we were over it. Splish splashed through the pond and out over a fallen branch! BOOM... HALF WAY!

9; a wooden table jumped nicely, to 10; a chair. Again, he backed off but got a firm leg on and we made it to the other side! Back up the hill to a hay-feeder at 11, one of my better efforts on the course and over a coffin and rail out at 12.

13; a house, I got a good shot at and we had a confident stride down to the rails and skinny nearing the end of the course. I rode the skinny like I meant business, nice short reins, closed leg... straight as a die, we soared it ... BLOODY GOOD BOY!

The next one I had doubts about but collected him up and nailed the skinny blue roll top on a dog leg to a corner. I got my line, tapped his shoulder with the stick and we flew them both. A gallop to the last, sailing over it and through the finish to come home 21 seconds under the time... 2.4 penalties to add to our dressage finishing on a 32.4!

WHAT A F*CKING HORSE... What a bloody tremendous result. Out of 43 in the section we came 3rd, got our Regional Final ticket and jumped another bloody DOUBLE CLEAR!

I literally cannot put into words how much today meant to me, how that bond we have that gets me so choked up, has conquered another outing in the most rewarding way. My horse is not easy to ride, he is by no means a confidence giver and all of his training is 7 years of putting up with my chubby arse guiding him through.

Today we proved that you don't have to be technically skilled or have a big bold jumping horse to go out an earn that placing. I feel I deserved it, I've been working hard, and I didn't let my jelly legs and last week's balls up get the better of me.

So, so much love for that little horse that will do anything for me, who answers my (sometimes, very vague) questions and makes my heart burst with love. I owe everything to him.

Massive thanks to Daddy Carrot for grooming and videoing. Thank you to you for your endless support and a big thank you to all the lovely people I met at Speetley today.

I cannot tell you how happy I am right now.... It'll be a few days before I hit the floor again that's for sure!

Love as always

Vic and Pat

Xxxx

~

Upping our game was going so well, preparing to succeed was also working for us rather than setting myself up to fail. I booked a jumping lesson the following week to keep my eye in and ended up pushing my limits once again. I was confidently jumping around a course, away from home, around 1.05m/1.10m and it didn't feel terrifying. This is the same horse and rider that didn't dare jump 60cms only two years ago. If ever you need proof that this is possible, you've got it right here. It is possible if you want it enough and boy, did I want it! I wasn't giving up and I was seriously going for it.

With this mindset, I entered my next event at Eland Lodge; another unfamiliar venue for us. But, Speetley had gone so well that I wasn't too afraid of the unknown anymore.

Only a few days had passed but these were days spent working away from home again, I was feeling really low for the first time in ages. I felt homesick and very run down and with anxiety never too far away, I lingered in this place of sadness and needed a kick up the arse.

**The sads...**

Five things to remember when you're feeling sad, when you feel beaten, when life doesn't seem to give you a break.

First thing, THIS IS TEMPORARY! It is not forever unless you choose for it to be. You have the power, you have the control, you can decide. You might need a hand out of the dirt, but that's why I'm here. It's just temporary, you won't be sad forever I promise.

Secondly, having the power... doesn't that feel great? You have the power; the right, the choice, to inhale, to wiggle your nose, to grab someone's bum (careful who you grab though, I don't want you on a sexual assault charge), you have the power. The choice to turn things around, to remove whatever it is making you sad, to deal with grief, to move forward... it might take time, it might not be instant, but YOU ARE IN CONTROL OF YOU.

Thirdly, find something positive to look forward to. Have a reason to smile, to get excited or to get out of bed. Have a passion, something you dare to dream about. Focus on it. Personally, I'm looking forward to being able to get shopping delivered from Morrison's now they've expanded their delivery zone, but you know... yours could be something much more brilliant.

Fourth, and perhaps most importantly, don't you dare linger on the negatives. Don't think twice about your grey hairs, cellulite or wrinkles... f*ck that sh*t! Stop worrying about things you cannot control, don't stress about the little things. Scrunch those things up into a ball and toss them out like a leaf in the wind. You are bloody brilliant; can you just take a second to make sure you know it!

Lastly, don't let other people stamp their dirty footprints on your life. You are wonderful, be true to who you are. People will respect you more for truth and honesty over lies and backstabbing any day. Don't compare yourself to anyone, you are so unique and so wonderful, you have greatness in you, we all do... let it out.

And there I was, at the end of another month, royally kicking my own arse. But it was too little, too late and I withdrew my entry from Eland.

**29th June 2018**

I've made the decision to withdraw from Saturday's event at Eland. It's going to be so hot, the ground will be firm, and I haven't ridden much this week. Pat doesn't jump well in the heat or on hard ground (roll back to Rackham last year) and a knock in confidence is not worth any amount of entry fee! My boy means the absolute world to me and that's what I keep in mind

~

In honesty, I had panic entered Eland as a last ditch attempt to get a Regional Final ticket and now that I got one at Speetley, I took the pressure off us. The ground **was** hard and those people that did run confirmed it for me. I made the right choice for us and I wasn't disappointed in myself for that. You need to do what's right for you and your horse and I have learnt that more than ever this year.

With no events planned for a few weeks, Carrot and I decided it was high time we had a little break away. Neither of us have down time very often, and with limited funds a holiday seemed like a luxury we could ill afford, but it was almost certainly worth it.

We flew to Spain, hired a car and stayed in a cheap B&B for a week in the sun. Something was different for us, I felt different. I felt content and happy and full of love. I also felt bloated, swollen in the breasts and adamant I was harbouring a bun in my oven.

This was the happiest I have been in such a long time, I had secretly pined to be pregnant for ages and I was beginning to worry that it might not happen for us. But, there I was in Spain for a whole week, refraining from too much alcohol and looking forward to getting home and doing a test to confirm what I was already so sure of.

## JULY 2018

## The Moment of Truth

I didn't even get as far as the plane doors when the worst thing imaginable happened. I just popped to the loo one last time before we left the hotel for home and there it was, the moment that my week of ridiculous happiness came careering down around my ears. I got my period. The swollen boobs, bloating and contentment was just pre-menstrual symptoms, and having not had those during my years of long term contraception, I had convinced myself I was pregnant.

I hadn't just convinced myself though, I was so happy about it too. And I don't think I have ever felt so much disappointment as I did sitting on the toilet that day. I didn't even tell Carrot about my initial suspicions, so it meant I also had to hide my state of crippling sadness and anguish from him too. I felt f*cking horrible. And I got so pissed on the plane on the way home that I slept the whole car journey back!

Horrible, horrible bloody female body trickery. My mind was all over the place and I certainly didn't feel nice and rested. Just anxious and back to convincing myself I had a defective womb! Great!

You shouldn't miss what you never had.  But I did. Box it away Vic, come on!

Back to throwing myself into competing, I guess!

So, I trundled out and went for a lesson with an old friend to try and get my missing mojo back.

**19th July 2018**

Do you ever just take a step back and think, look and evaluate?

Today, I drove my horse, in MY little, slightly rusty horsebox through town and all the traffic (which would have scared me sh*tless before) for a lesson with one of my best friends.

Tonight, I have just showered and changed after my lesson in her beautiful home, and right now she's cooking me dinner. I don't have half the facilities, the beautifully soft White Company furnishings or impeccable taste that she has. Nor do I have quite the eye for a horse or the riding ability, but we are the best of friends and it makes anything tangible invisible.

She had taught me so much today. Not just about my riding but about how lucky we all are in so many ways. In my lesson we barely scratched the surface, but a true friend can give you very honest feedback without you taking offence. A true friend wants you to succeed as much as you want it.

This particular friend highlighted pivotal balance issues and tension in my thigh which is almost certainly the reason why I feel so scared. Being out of balance and grabbing hold of my horse makes him panic, which makes me panic, which makes me grab and grip... vicious circle huh?!

Now I know what the problems and areas of weakness are, I can work hard to fix them.

Tonight, I am grateful for good horses, for good wine and for very good friends.

~

You need times like this to get your perspective back and true friends like these don't come around that often. If you have these people in your life, cherish them. Message them often just asking how they are, be there for them and they will be there for you in return. **LESSON 6: YOU NEED GOOD PEOPLE**. I think I've said it once before… Surround yourself with people that either couldn't give a sh*t, ones that would give their last sh*t to see you succeed, or the ones that don't know what sh*t you're doing. Forget about the ones that drag you down and give all your time and energy to the ones that make you feel as brilliant as you really are.

~

If I'm totally honest, July went so fast. I was away with work again and my heart was battered. I felt like hibernating, but I had entered Frickley BE at the end of the month, so I kept slogging forwards. It came up so quickly and I'm not sure my heart was really in it looking back;

**NUMBER 4 : Frickley Park BE90**

So, only my 3rd affiliated event of the season (can't quite believe I'm saying this when it's nearly August!) happened yesterday at Frickley Park!

I've been consciously trying to lighten up about things and try to enjoy having fun with my horse instead of piling on pressure and being a miserable cockwomble. This was the one and only aim of yesterday... no wobbles allowed!

Daddy Carrot had to work with it being a Friday so Auntie Smurph, who is a teacher and on school holidays stepped in as chief in charge of calming my nerves and helping me out.

We arrived in plenty of time for my 9.48am dressage (NEWSFLASH: no toilet happenings!) and with a 3 hour gap between that and show jumping, in almost 30 degrees, I'd packed plenty of water for Pat and stupidly decided that would be a good time to walk the cross country.

I collected my number and plaited (still no toilet happenings!) feeling remarkably calm and actually enjoying the day. At this point, time tends to just slip away so quickly and by the time I got on, I only had 20 minutes until I was in the ring!

Now, on the way we had rain, a miracle really, but it meant the hard ground was then lined with a film of dampness. I put in medium pointy studs on advice of my friend Kathryn who is very experienced, and that seemed to do the job of keeping him upright.

For anyone that doesn't know, the dressage warm up is my biggest fear. The time when he's usually fresh as a badger's arse, most likely to throw some killer shapes and send me flying through the air onto my head and potentially leaving in an ambulance. Today though, he was seriously awesome!

I didn't take up a contact AT ALL until I had to go down to ring, I let him lollop about and I just enjoyed it... WHAT A BLOODY DIFFERENCE!

I went into the test calm and happy, I felt like it deserved one of our better marks. He was forward, on the aids, happy and so was I! I was enjoying cantering my last 20m circle so much that I forgot to trot resulting in a beep from the judge and 2 marks added but I couldn't have cared less!

I was absolutely over the moon to not feel frightened at an event, I could have gone home happy there and then!

On seeing the course photos the night before, I knew what I was in for and because we've done this event twice before, my course walk was purely to check the going. The organisers had worked so hard to water as much as possible, but the first section of the course wasn't filling me with joy.

It got better though, and I decided to see how he jumped in the show jumping as to whether I would run him cross country.

By the time I jumped at 1pm, it was unbelievably hot, and Pat was really trying his best. He has never jumped that well on hard ground, but I think the course was on the best going of the whole show ground! In the ring, fences came and went like they were nothing and 1-5 jumped really well off a beautiful big stride. We had an unfortunate rail at the back of the double at 5 and sadly, I took the sh*ttest line known to human kind around a bend to 6.

He slipped a bit, lost his footing and I just took my leg off on the turn to ease out of it. But the jump was upon us and with no leg on, the little bugger stopped. I couldn't get cross, it was entirely my fault and we came around a second time no problem.

The wheels fell off a little bit, having the next fence down but we finished over the last two brilliantly.

I came out of the ring happy and that's all that mattered to us.

16 to add to our dressage which was an unusually high 36 (reflective of the section, as we were in the top 10 dressage scores), on paper the cr*ppest day we've had, but I didn't feel disappointed.

Now, with the heat and the way he lost a bit of confidence in the show jumping, I went and withdrew. Bailed out, lost my bottle, stormed off because of a bad score... or, quit while I was ahead! We had achieved everything I set out to in the first 20 minutes of our dressage warm up, so I would have left happy regardless.

My little horse has nothing to prove, we didn't need to gallop on hard ground for 6 minutes on a hot day. There's always another day but, my goodness; there's no other horse like him.

We left much cooler than we would have been, and we left happy. That's what's important.

I had the best day and I know to some I might have failed, but inside my head and my heart and the legs of my horse, we won today.

Here's to rain, moving forward and our next outing!!

~

And that was it, another month over. A massive disappointing non-pregnancy, a hugely expensive combined training show and nothing much to show for July at all. I felt a bit flat and kept dwelling on how much I came on last season compared to this one. Something had to change, and I was going to have to make it happen!

## AUGUST 2018

## Time Flies!

**5th August 2018**

Yesterday we ventured back to Epworth Equestrian for their Combined Training show. For anyone not familiar with this term, it's just like Eventing only much less expensive and no death phase (cross country) to worry about!

After bailing out at Frickley last Monday, I figured I might just take up knitting or cross stitch. But with Pat still lounging about in the field and some irritating fire for eventing in my groin, I knuckled down to setting things straight!

I actually sought advice of the Internet first, just like I would for illness diagnosis, and I received some excellent advice from one lady in particular. I learnt that to get consistent low-mid 20s dressage scores, I need to:

Have much more pizzazz and the trot needs more power!

The canter needs to be uphill and forward

Pat needs to be in front of the vertical

I need to look like I'm doing much less (ie STOP NAGGING!!)

Maintain accuracy of all the movements

Ride the centre line like you mean business

Improve the halt

Basically, improve EVERYTHING!! But above all of this, and no one in particular pointed it out, I've got to stop riding for survival and ride for the win. Up until now I have only gone to a show expecting to come home in one piece. That's not enough anymore if you actually would like to do well, which I think I do!

So yesterday I made some very drastic mental and physical changes. It was a turning point for us both.

First thing, I learnt the test and actually bothered to hire an arena and practice it! I also put spurs on (in practice too) because I often find that I'm nagging all the time with my big fat legs which are as useful as a wasp in my wine. The spurs helped me keep stiller and ask once rather than a hundred nags!

I carried my hands up and forwards but kept a shorter rein, kicking him up into that uphill feeling hand means his nose doesn't dip behind the bridle and he's rarely ever on the forehand!! Winner!

I prepared movements better, I also pushed the canter out of my rocking horse, "going nowhere" pace that I love to sit to, but that doesn't score points!! Having the shorter rein and better connection meant it wasn't too unbalanced either!

I will also add, that I've stripped him of the calmer. Yep, I've said it out loud now! No more calmer, not the powder in his tea or show day syringes! If I want pizzazz, you can't piss on the spark and I've spent 2 years pissing on those sparks for fear of the flames getting out of hand! TIME TO MAN UP!

I rode the best test I feel like I've ever ridden. It was BE92 (my upcoming RF test). My halt definitely could be better, and my accuracy could improve, but the 74% it received meant these changes worked and would have meant a 26, reflective of the day because out of about 40 competitors we were the highest of all of them by a decent margin!

A quick change and down to the jumping, the course was long and winding but luckily, I chose to jump 80cms after recent stopping at both Frickley and the disaster last time we came to Epworth. It was a day for confidence and trying new techniques not proof we can jump big jumps!

We jumped clear after a lucky knock of number two that didn't fall... We went clear, which felt AMAZING!

He won the class by almost 10 points and I felt, and still feel, absolutely elated. Hard work, practice and knowing when and how to take and use advice has meant WINNING!

I've been riding for 25 years on hundreds of different horses (no exaggeration). I have experience, feel, knowledge and a very capable horse to ride BUT if you don't have the capacity to learn, to be humble and to hold your hands up when you hit a wall, that experience and ability is worth jack sh*t.

This week has been enlightening, my red rosette is one of my proudest yet and I will keep on trying in the same way.

Thank you all so, so much for your endless support and help. For being there for me and Pat, to those people that popped over for a chat and a cheeky cigarette, thank you all.

Love as always, Vic and Pat

Xxxx

~

What a difference these little changes can make. I learnt so much about how differently things could go if you actually go out with the intention of doing well. I feel ridiculous and as though I'm pointing out the obvious, but if you want to win; you can. You just have to want to, and change things in order to make that happen.

Things on the non-horsey (pregnancy) front were definitely not following the same pattern. I wanted that more than I've ever wanted any bloody red rosette and all I had was red visitor of a different kind. It was beginning to affect me more than I realised.

I was longing with all my heart to conceive and it wasn't happening.

**9th August 2018**

November marks a year of "not, not trying", calling it that seems much less threatening, and part of me thought it would have happened long before now. Yes, I am aware that just 10 months "clean" after 13 years of medicinal contraception is absolutely nothing, but I can't help the way I feel.

I am soon to be 33 and very happily married to my second husband, we are *coughs* active in that way too and both know the timing is right.

Every month when my boobs are sore and twice the size, and my body teases me by throwing my cycle out one or two days, I feel elated, hopeful and so happy. Then, just a day later, totally bloody shattered when I get my b*stard period that I don't f*cking want. They don't call it 'the curse' for nothing!

I want to be f*cking pregnant. But this is the trouble, I want it too much. I want it more than a spin around Badminton or possibly the end to world hunger… and that's totally f*cking selfish too!

I'm sure there are people that will read this who have been 'not, not trying' for much longer or can't have their own babies, and all I have learnt so far is, I can quite imagine how you feel. You are amazing though, in your own right, with or without a baby. You are wonderful and don't ever forget it. Don't lose hope, please don't. You never know what life will bring, you never know what is around the corner. Don't plan too far ahead, live for now and be the happiest you can every single day.

~

And for once, I took my own advice! I stopped fretting as soon as I wrote this down in my diary. The power of a diary, I will keep one for as long as I live.

Back to business! With my Regional Final only 2 weeks away I decided we probably needed another run before hand to keep our eye in, and so I entered an unaffiliated event back at Epworth, just a nice local one to give us a spin out.

## NUMBER 5: Epworth Unaffiliated 80cms

Now, for anyone wondering. Yes, I have my BE90 Regional Final at Shelford in 2 weeks and yes, I know I did the 80cm class today but I want my horse's confidence to blossom, I want him happy and keen and I also want to enjoy it too. Epworth was a challenging track last time, so I decided that instead of fearing the full up 90, I would have much more fun jumping 80 and letting him have a go at finding some balls too!

I've been quite slack this week on the riding front, mainly because the ground is rock hard and also because my lorry broke down on Thursday, pre-jumping lesson! (It's fixed...sort of!!) I had a quick run through of my test, but I gave him yesterday off and a pretty easy week all things considered.

We set off, (Wimpy Wagon started up like a peach) arriving in plenty of time to let Pat chill his beans and for Carrot and me to walk the course.

Within two minutes of course walking my belly burst out of my breeches through a zip fly which apparently, could no longer contain my sizeable gut!! Lucky, I had a pin spare! It was a nice course however, and the guys at Epworth have some excellent covered going!! I was happy!

Without calmer syringing or his daily powder, I was surprised that when I plaited and tacked up ready for dressage and walked down to the warm up, he was so chilled. He was lazy if anything, but we were having FUN! We were enjoying the dressage warm up! I didn't spoil it by picking him up too much and in the ring and it showed. He did a sweet test and got the second best mark of the whole class for a 30.3, it could have had more spark, but I was thrilled regardless.

Back at the box and a quick change for show jumping. I was really happy, content even. No nerves, no grizzly old baggage, I was even nice to my husband. I watched a few go, learnt the course and warmed up.

There were not many people going clear and Epworth is renowned for having a spooky jumping arena (we've had a few disasters here too). I walked him in like we owned the joint, no flapping, no rushing, just mooching about like we were on a trip to Skegness having chips on the sea front. Popped up into canter and lolloped our way around the first few and he started TAKING CONTROL! My horse; that spooky, backward thinking fella, picked up the bit and started taking ME to the jumps! I nearly soiled myself; out of shock, not fear this time! It was sensational, I've wanted him to pull me into a jump for 6 years and today was his day. It was his day to start a journey and what a magnificent one it will be.

So, with only one unlucky rub of a shady jump at number 6. We headed out of the ring smiling our biggest smiles EVER!

Getting ready for cross country, the nerves were there, but manageable. I got us both ready and we set off to pop a few practice jumps. The lovely starter man said we could go straight through, but knowing how excited Pat gets in the start box of doom, I asked the man if I could settle him in there as good practice before he sent us away. I settled him and away we went!

Determined not to gun it too fast, I let the rhythm just come as he felt comfortable, like a medium to fast canter I suppose. The first fence was a bit sticky, he wasn't going to stop but he did hesitate, and I kept a firm leg on to number two; a box fence with holes in it. He looked but again I was right there to catch him, soaring it and cantering away round the sweeping turn to 3; a table and 4 and 5; two log piles. I let him take the lead, he decided to go himself... HE TOOK ME IN!

I wiped tears of joy from my eyes before number 6a&b, two narrower jumps, b being quite gappy and bright... he nailed it! Bang on stride like an absolute pro! Crikey I need to stop pride making my eyes leak when I'm going around!

Next, a house which he also took on all guns blazing, and onto the carrot table which, never getting complacent, he needed my help at. I just put a bit of extra leg on and we sailed it.

Round the back of the woods and over three more jumps on a new track none of which a problem, and back out into the field to 11, he was back to being in charge! Pulled me in and I loved it, whooping and cheering to the next! 12; a pipe and flowers jumped well, onto the water which he usually likes to come back to trot for. Not today my friends! He cantered through it and out over a previously problematic wishing well like it was nothing!

A leg stretch up to the top of the field over 15; a roll top and bounding off the drop, he soared 16 like it wasn't even there! Through the woods I began tiring, I need to get fitter! We steadied up a little bit but out the trees and two from home, we both whooped with joy!!!

The last two fences came and went as we burst over the finish line of the most amazing round and day out eventing I have EVER had.

Turns out we went over 30 secs too fast! Giving us a penalty of 8.8tf to add. We still finished 5th in our section and got the most amazing PINK rosette!

Placings, numbers, prizes and records mean absolutely Jack sh*t if you're not out there having the absolute time of your life. It's all meaningless if there's no passion, no love for the sport or appreciation of anything other than the win.

For us, it's not about winning.

For us, it's being the best team we can be.

Today, we were the best, Pat was the best and he continues to surprise me with his big lion heart. Growing his confidence is more rewarding than anything I've ever done.

Thank you to my wonderful support team, my darling Daddy Carrot and to you, for your encouragement and love, it means a lot.

Love as always, Vic & Pat

Xxx

~

I don't think my pre Regional Final run could have gone much better than that. I was determined to not let the nerves get to me like last year's version of events. But for some reason I wasn't as in control as I'd have liked. Throughout the season you get to pick up qualifying results (approx top 3 in your section) which mean you collect 'tickets' that deem you eligible for a RF at that level. At the final you have to come in the top 20% to get through to the championship held at Badminton alongside the main international event there in May. And as I am the LEAST competitive person EVER, I started to feel very uneasy about this. The lead up wasn't what I hoped for and nor did the day go how I thought it would in my head. So many times, I visualised how I would feel getting that Badminton place. Much like I visualise what I would do with the lottery jackpot. But the reality is, I'm still skint and I'm not going to Badminton… not yet anyway!

**MITSUBISHI MOTORS CUP – REGIONAL FINAL RF90**

Unfortunately, my usual preparation in the run up to an event was scuppered because I had to stay away for work Monday to Wednesday last week. It also marked my job handover and official unemployment, so I expect my mind and nerves weren't helped by this pressure either.

Saturday, I walked the course with one of my Team Wimpy chums, Becki and I felt comfortable that there was nothing on the course that was dressed with flowers or seemed to be too scary! Result! That also meant the fight for a Badminton slot would rest solely on the other two phases! Heading home I was riddled by palpitations but not feeling too horrible. I got everything ready, rode through my test one last time and got an early (non booze filled) night!

I woke up to my 4.45am alarm and got out the house by 5.20am. With no time for bowel emptying or feeling too scared, we set off.

15 minutes into the journey, the nerves came. I used to feel them the month before, then just the week before, this year I've narrowed the time spent panicking down to the last few hours. I'm hoping to eventually get rid of them all together one day! But today, I had the WORST nerves I think I have EVER felt in my whole life.

Worse than waiting for my divorce to be accepted, worse than when Pat got cast and injured at Talland; the worst nerves of my life hit me like a train.

We pulled over, so I could use the toilet and eventually made it to Shelford and their line of portaloos. My body was a mess, it was making me physically sick which I don't think has ever happened before. I felt cold, shivery and light headed. My hands struggled to do up my tack and the tightness in my chest was making me panic. I wanted to cry and not just out of nerves, I felt desperately sad about how I felt. I thought after Epworth, we had turned a huge corner but the pressure of having to be competitive was making me feel this awful fear of disappointment.

I got on and warmed up, he was so lovely, not a single spook or salmon fish impression. In the test he was far lazier than I'd have liked, and I have learnt that this is penalised heavily in eventing. But I kept him out in the frame just like I'd been practicing, I thought it deserved around a 35 so guess what... I actually breathed for the first time all morning! I had resigned myself to never getting through on that score, you'd need sub 30 to be in with a chance and I was so happy.

The pressure was off, I laughed all the way back to the box at how stupid I'd been! I hugged Pat and apologised to Daddy Carrot and proceeded to enjoy the morning eventing as much as I could!

I went show jumping with the biggest grin on my face! We warmed up and chatted away to a load of lovely people, and in the ring, I just breathed and had FUN! He never jumps well in the ring at Shelford and he did have a couple of spooks! He was giving the fences a lot of room which made some of the distances quite short and deep resulting in rolling 3 poles, but I didn't care one bit! He was bouncing, and I was so happy to be out there having fun!

I also learnt that my dressage score was a 35 but not at all that bad looking at the other scores, definitely top half but certainly not what we are actually capable of on our best day.

Down in the XC warm up I was feeling excited to get going! I decided to test out wearing my stopwatch today too! And here we were, popping the practice jumps with no spooking, just me and my boy having fun!

In the box, I got counted down and actually remembered to start the speedo!! A short run to a kind log at number 1 which he boinged over no bother, to number 2; a box with milk churns on, he looked but I was there to catch him, and we bounded down to the step up at 3. We rounded the corner before it in a steady canter, probably not as bouncy as it should have been and then it happened...

He fell.

He misjudged the height, scrambled and stumbled and eventually scraped his way up. He's so good at steps that I just usually hold the mane and wait, but today he was left a bit sore and feeling very frightened. I trotted a few strides and he felt ok so popped him back up to canter for the chair at 4.

He stopped.

He was frightened after the step, and I don't blame him. But I needed to show him it was okay. We circled, I gave him a big pat and we flew over it, cantering our way down to a brush at 5 and a little log, number 6. Both of these we had a sticky jump, but I knew I had the rest of the course to make him realise it was okay again.

7; a roll top, he started to get a bit more confidence, splashing through the water and over the log at 8, he lost momentum but WHAT A HORSE! He pinged over it and galloped down to 9 and 10 two sets of rails in the hedge lines, ping ping!!! He was flying now, back in his stride!

Down at the double of pipes for 11 and into the woods, we were screaming with joy! He was pulling me into the palisade at 12 and we were flying once more!

The jump I got at 13, the straw bale pheasant feeder... was one of the best jumps I've ever had! He took me in and I sobbed with pride! 14 was a skinny house which he jumped well and onto the brush going back into the woods. No problem for him, he was heading home now, and he felt full of beans!

Pop pop! Out over the yellow pipes in the woods and down a step which I steadied him up for. A long gallop to the final brush and log which he was seriously keen for and through the finish flags!

I couldn't have been happier with how we finished our day, I was and still am, absolutely ecstatic. He was amazing and grew in confidence with every jump after his fall. I helped him, and he actually responded and what a feeling that is. Better than a Badminton qualification or rosette that's for sure!

He did manage to take a good bit of fur and skin off a hind leg, but I washed it really well and put some antiseptic cream on it before we took him home.

I grabbed a burger, my dressage sheet and my photos and headed home, so stupidly happy for what it might look like on paper.

Our dressage of 35 wouldn't have been enough anyway, 33 would have but that's hindsight. With 12 jumping penalties to add, a stop XC and a few time faults we ended the day at the very bottom of the most elite of 90 sections. And guess what? I was probably as happy (if not more) than those people that qualified.

It's not about winning for us, I say it often, but it really isn't. I don't want to be a disappointment and that's what got to me this morning. I have sponsors and all you amazing people that I want to do well for. But the truth is; I can't consistently do well, it's not reality and anyone that thinks they can are deluded. I want you all to know that you can win even if you aren't placed first. I've never felt like such a winner than I do having my horse bounding into a jump on his own accord and that's what matters.

I could blame the hideous weather, the comments on my sheet not being accurate, I could have ridden for the clear show jumping or walloped him over that chair from a standstill but that isn't us. We value smiles over prizes and points.

Massive huge thanks to all of you, who continue to support me even though our results might not be the best, my riding might not be perfect and without a string of top horses... you are all amazing. Thank you xxxxx

Here's to the next one!!

~

And that's the point isn't it? You are on your own path. If you want to jump small jumps, do that. If you want to jump big ones, that's fine too. If all you want is a hack to the pub, bloody well enjoy that. If dressage is for you, that's cool. Please don't feel you need to prove anything to anyone. **LESSON 7: MAKE YOUR OWN RULES**. It's your life, your horse and your sanity... do what makes YOU happy.

I wasn't massively pleased with my progression this year when I compared it to last year. But what hope did I have, the ground was too wet, then it was too hard, then I got pissed, the lorry broke down, I got nervous again… seriously, no wonder I hadn't stepped back up to jumping 1m classes. I was being too hard on myself and decided enough was enough. It was just fun, fun, fun from this point onwards!

## September 2018

## Falling into place

My next event was at Frickley Park again and this time it wasn't too hot, hard or wet! In fact, the going was great, I knew the challenges on the course and with Daddy Carrot coming along to kick my back side into shape, we got on with the job!

**NUMBER 7: Frickley Park BE90**

So, here we are again... on the eve of an event and having just walked the course, I didn't feel horrendous. Certainly, nowhere near as bad as my last event at Shelford. I put so much pressure on myself there and I didn't enjoy a single bit of that feeling.

Frickley was all about having FUN as a priority.

My dressage was at 8.18am and I was set to be finished all three phases by 10.30, so only two small gins in the pub on our traditional Friday night drink and we were home and in bed by 10pm all set for our 4.30am alarm!

The feeling that usually hits me "how easy would it be to just withdraw?" when the alarm sounds wasn't there today. I sprung out of bed and hopped into my breeches and out the door feeling almost excited for the first time in ages! We loaded Pat and set off on our 1hr45 journey. Made a pit stop for coffee and toilet necessities, and after a short directional malfunction we were parked up at Frickley albeit running a little behind schedule! I plaited in record time (about 3 and a half minutes!) and got ready whilst Daddy Carrot trotted off to get my number and pay the start fee. Minutes later we were heading down to dressage with only 20 minutes to go before I was in!

I stupidly gave him a bit of the calmer syringe when we stopped at the services, just like in times gone by. I thought it would help me with our recent show jumping stops but alas, it just confirmed what I already knew; that it just can't be relied upon and sometimes creates more tension and excitement in him (and was probably the cause of my last two years of fear to mount at shows)!

He was a total d*ck; buzzy, wired and I was back feeling scared again. I will happily admit that the calmer was a big mistake on my part and one I will not make again. Settled and in the test, the same one I've done pretty much all season, I went bloody wrong! I got the sodding horn of shame, I knew instantly what I'd done by cantering in the wrong place, but I gathered myself, redid the bit I screwed up and finished the test.

Walking back to change for jumping, the rain fell heavier and heavier... I felt anxious about slipping and skidding about in the ring and when I finally got my act together and got back on, my legs had turned to wiggly tentacles of uselessness!

We only had a few to go before us so I popped a couple of cross poles, knocked down an upright or two and saw a crappy stride to an oxer and we were in!

He spooked at the first fence, but we made it, despite having studs in, he had a little skid in front of the second and just ground to a stop! B*LLOCKSSSSS! I forgot to do anything again, I sat there like a wet fish on a soggy day... I did NOTHING! D*ckhead Vic, you really, really are!

I circled and rode like I actually wanted him to do it and guess what... he did it! I then got my arse in gear and rode my very best hunting style round, growling and shouting and kicking like stink. It was not pretty but he was jumping so well! We actually came out with only 1 time penalty thanks to my forward riding so that was 5 to add to our dressage score and left us sitting in the top 3!

A quick change and we were in the XC warm up with 20 minutes! I was just aiming for getting around, building his confidence back up at the steps after his fall at Shelford and if we made it to the end, well that would have been a bonus!

The starter man was so nice, but his 3...2...1, still made me want to set him on fire and chuck him in a bush!

The first fence came up really quickly, barely 100 yards from the box; it was kind and we sailed it confidently and galloped I'm up to a wooden flower wall at number 2. He backed off and we hit a duff stride, but we were over it and it made me buck my ideas up a bit!

There was a roll top that I really had to ride him at, spooky little sod! Flying over that, I pulled out left and cornered into my planned line for a double of offset hedge-topped boxes. WOW! What a jump we got at those, he locked on and understood what I was asking! Result!

5 was the hedge and rails which he jumped so big, it felt like we were in the air forever, such an amazing feeling! I wish I'd got a picture of that, I was seriously beaming! 6a&b; a wooden box jump and down quite a large step, he pinged the jump and confidently flew off the step pulling me down the hill towards 7! He was loving it, and so was I!

7 was a white house which jumped fine, to 8; the trakehener. I pushed for a big bold stride to that, so he wouldn't look into the bottom and it worked, eyes up, legs on and we soared! 9 was up a bank and just one stride down to and a wooden palisade, pinging over like a little dear, my first question on the course was looming so I shortened him up ready for a skinny log and step up for 10.

He came back to me well and popped the log, I held the mane and kept the rhythm and this time he pinged up the step no bother at all! Huge big squeal and pat on the neck and we were off!

Over the rail at 11 and a lovely wall at 12, my only two let up fences on the course. We hooked right into the woods, left and right again to a military style rail with hessian sacks under it. He backed right off it, ground to what was almost a stop and I had to think fast. I growled, kicked and waggled my whip and he hopped over it like a little stag! Bloody spooky sh*t bag! And complacent jockey! This did not bode well for the double of skinny offset logs at 14a&b.

I brought the canter right back and made it VERY obvious what the question was, he answered correctly and nailed both parts! I've never screamed as loud or felt such pride, I apologise to the spectators for my monster scream of "You are a F*€king GOOD BOY", what a bloody horse though!

Into the water at a trot because I literally didn't care about anything other than how amazing he was! We popped out over the roll top and bounced down to that hideous green and white corner! I collected, steered and he thought about running out, but there was nowhere for him to go. I held fast, and he jumped it bang on! A hard left turn to the flower box skinny that he's always had a look at and just like before, I held him securely together and true as a die, he pinged over it!

At this point I thought it had felt quite a fast round so I let him cruise a bit over the last two fences. We flew the flowered wall and saw a duff stride at the last, but we were clear and through the flags, screaming with pride! I hopped off and undid his girth and nosebands and hugged him so tight! We did it, we did it!

He was so unbelievably amazing, just the ability for him to understand what I ask and agree with what I'm telling him to do. I've taught him to jump these jumps, I've made mistakes too don't get me wrong, but what a feeling it is when it's right. Having a horse understand what is required at each testing obstacle and do exactly what is asked; it's just amazing. I will never take for granted how magnificent my horse is, how brave he and I can be when we are working as a team. We have something so special and I adore every little inch of him.

Back at the box, we washed him down and settled him back on the van with a big haynet and plenty of polos and sugar lumps. We went to buy photos and peeped in to find that I had actually gone a bit too slow and should I have not "cruised" home on the XC, we would have been in the top 5! Alas, 11th place for us but who gives a fat rats ass?! Not me!! My horse makes me feel like a winner every time!

Here's to the next one, the final one of 2018!

Love as always, Vic and Pat

Xxxxx

~

**"You always look so happy when you're riding…."**

I hear this without fail at least once a month sometimes more than once a day. I don't edit out the pictures that show my gurning, scared sh*tless face either. The truth is, I am happy and more to the point, why does that surprise people?

Despite how elated I was when I came back down to earth after Frickley, nothing was going to come close to how happy I was about to be.

You see, this doesn't start massively jovial because I was down in West Sussex for a few days to hand over my main income to a new in-house employee. Now, I had been with this group of companies for over 3 years and built this job roll up from nothing. The brands were mine, the websites were mine and I felt very out of sorts handing all of it over to a new lady who, with a background in law and professional services, didn't really seem fit for the very outgoing role. It was out of my hands, but I left with a heavy heart, nonetheless. I had become very fond and possessive of my position there and I didn't like the thought of them managing without me either.

Throughout my marketing career spanning the last ten years, I have had some great jobs. But none have got under my skin like this one did. I was obsessed. I think it's the main reason I wanted to start my own company, I wanted to feel ownership of something that was actually mine! But let me tell you; it's not the same when it's yours!

Anyway, I was down in West Sussex doing the final handover and as always on my trips down south, I like to try and catch up with my local friends. This trip was no different, I met up with my friend Linda for dinner.

Linda and I first met at a riding club training day. I took Pat there for the first time when I joined my new club Wey Valley RC. Linda ran the training there and she was so welcoming. At the time, I was riding and schooling a few horses for people for extra cash, recently Pat had gone out on loan because of my sh*tty financial situation and I was chatting to Linda about this when the subject first came up.

Linda had a horse in sales livery. This horse; a full thoroughbred mare, was costing far more per month on livery than she was hoping to get for selling her. So, what did I do? I offered to take her on the same arrangement but with no sales livery fee and went to have a look at her!

I remember going into the barn and seeing this little black horse, she wasn't really anything flashy and full thoroughbred, so naturally on the thin and stressy side! But, my goodness I love a thoroughbred and after everything Linda had told me about her, I thought she would be fun to have around. 2 weeks later, she turned up!

Her name was Pea. And she filled the huge Pat shaped hole in my heart far quicker than I could have wished for. She was ballsy, determined and knew her own mind, but she was also insanely loyal, with the biggest trusting heart I'd ever known.

Linda covered all of her costs and I did the work. Win win. I had her jumping courses, took her to shows and cross country schooling. I did all the Riding Club team events and qualified for the Festival of the Horse and the show jumping championships. She jumped clear so many times I lost count and brought me so much happiness when I needed it the most.

I vividly recall our first and only affiliated event. The rain pelted for days beforehand making trenches in the dressage arena, particularly down the centre line. She wasn't keen on this part at all never mind in the trenches with it p*ssing rain into her face! We had an unfortunate pole down in the show jumping and headed for cross country sodden, but really up for it! She flew out of the start box and tackled everything I asked of her, including THE WRONG FENCES! I jumped a fence that was part of the novice class the next day. I thought it felt big, but she didn't think so and cleared it by a mile! Sadly, we learnt of our elimination crossing the finish line and really didn't care either! She was AMAZING!!

I never felt nervous on her, not once. She taught me to trust a horse again and taught me to love riding just like I used to. I was totally smitten. She absolutely hated being stabled and regularly pulled a fast once pretending to have colic… see me dashing like lightening to the yard only for her to make a miraculous recovery as soon as I arrived! Minx! I could never really get her that round and soft on the flat either, but I didn't care! We were having so much fun.

When Pat came back under his naughty cloud from being out on loan, and having Pea there to restore my confidence, I was torn between them. Pea was so good, even Carrot rode her. But I was struggling for time and Pat was always left at home, with me choosing to ride Pea over him anywhere I went. He frightened me, and she didn't, it was a no-brainer. But he was my horse, she wasn't. It was him I should have sold, it was him that made me cry at night, not her, not my lovely little Pea. But alas I was drowning in it all, I had the conversation with Linda about finding her a new home and we did just that.

A friend of a friend tried her and a week later took her on full loan. Just like that, it was Pat and I on our own again. This was good for Linda as there were now no costs involved and the lady seemed really nice, so I was happy (ish) too!

That was the last I heard from Pea for over two years. I felt guilty asking after her, I'm not sure why. I did get wind of her having problems with soundness and sore back problems, followed by ulcers and treatment for them. You never really know what goes on when you just Facebook stalk instead of actually asking! But I knew Pea wasn't right. I also knew Linda took her back at some point too. And there she stayed, Feral Beryl-ing in the field for the next two years!

Linda did try and ride her a couple of times and had a physio fella out to look at her a few times too, but she is such a strong-willed mare. Pea knows exactly how to tell you something isn't right and so she was just kept as a pet by Linda, who would feed her horses over herself any day!

Now, roll forward to our evening in West Sussex. We sat having dinner and amongst other conversations; Linda explains that she is no longer in a position to keep Pea as a costly field ornament. She didn't have the time, the money or much hope that she would ever come sound enough to ride and aside from finding her a home as a companion (that doesn't like being on her own, weaves like Billy-o and fakes colic), the option of her being put to sleep, flashed across both of our faces.

It really was the easiest decision I have ever had to make.

"I'll take her."

There wasn't any question in the matter.

I messaged Carrot, he was happy too. We were both absolutely delighted to be getting her home. Both babies reunited. I was happier than I had been for many, many years that night.

## October 2018

## When one door closes…

In order to end my mismatched season on the best note possible, I decided to go out at 80cms and have an absolute ball with my horse on our last run.

I didn't feel embarrassed or ashamed about dropping down a level, he wouldn't notice, and I would just feel a little bit more confident ending my season this way. I've spent more money on lessons this year than events and I feel like our show jumping has come on so much because of that. I also feel more capable in this area and now the weaknesses are shining through in other places that I need to work on!

I had also driven the 200mile round trip to meet Linda half way form West Sussex with Pea, and she was out in the field with Pat looking very content indeed. I booked her feet in to be done, had my lovely physio booked to take a look and felt very happy to love two horses so much.

It was having Pea in the field with Pat that made me realise just how wrong it was with Bender. Although I loved him, he really didn't fit in with our very laid back life here. My horses live outdoors 24/7 and I'm not sure Sir Bentley was up for that. You have to listen to them, be able to read what they are trying to tell you. Bender is very happy on a bigger yard with hustle and bustle. Pat fits in with most situations as long as I'm around (and food is around) and Pea is definitely an outdoorsy girl. Routine and having them happy and content are so important to me.

Once Pea had had the once over, I waited with bated breath for a couple of days before popping her on the lunge to see how level she was.

To my utter amazement, she looked totally fine! So, I started leading out off Pat for a few rides to get her strength up before I sat my chubby arse on her tiny body!

But, back to his Nibs… We were there, the time had come, it was the last event of the season already, I was determined to make it a fun one, but as always, things never turn out quite how you want them to!

**THE FINAL ONE: Norton Disney BE80.**

This is most certainly the hardest event report I've had to write all season. Even now, the morning after, I'm still so emotional about it.... it's a sport, a hobby damn it! Deep breath, here goes....

We spent the week hacking, running through my test and the usual. Nothing out of the ordinary and as we had stepped down to the 80 as a last confidence building run of the season, I didn't stress too much that we hadn't got out for a jump anywhere.

Now, I also entered the 80 because I am teaching all day today (Saturday) and Sunday's I can't really do (nerves, husband commitments), so it was either the 80 or the 100 on the Friday! Daddy Carrot took the day off and we trundled down to Norton Disney for our 1pm dressage and to walk the course beforehand.

The course was fine, we had loads of time too. We sat in the sunshine, just the three of us, drank tins of pop and I reflected on how lucky I felt... It really was lovely, but the nerves were lingering there somewhere.

I warmed up with the most awful pain in my nether regions. That one you get when you're greeted by a sodding period the day before a show, the one that not only reminds you that you're still not pregnant but also the one that means beige breeches are risking dark red leakage!

The pain was from a very unfortunately positioned string, one that I couldn't fix whilst on a horse and one that rubbed my skin so raw it felt like I'd been massaged by a cheese grater... anyway.... *ahem*!

I got on with it and in the arena, he was a total tit. I struggled to get him down towards the judges' car and the struggled to hold him together as he wanted to run from it! Either way, I wasn't thrilled with the outcome and thought I deserved about a 33.

With the string issue resolved, I changed tack and warmed up for the jumping. This has been my absolute weakest area for years and whilst I can't afford loads of training or many jumps to have at home, I've worked hard in my monthly lessons and practiced getting a good canter on the flat too.

In the warmup he felt a bit flat, but I like that, "flat-Pat" doesn't scare the living sh*t out of me like "buzzy-in-the-ring-Pat" does.

In we went, and he brightened up somewhat. Instead of soiling myself and clinging on, I used the energy to push forward and he was flying. A positive canter makes the world of difference for us and it certainly did today... WE WENT F*CKING CLEAR!

I properly welled up and felt seriously proud. My husband looked at me with that admiration I can't even put into words. That, right there, that was the proudest moment of my 2018 season.

We also learnt that in a section of dressage scores in the late 30's, by some miracle I was on a 29! Putting us in first place.... by a solid margin after that wonderful clear round.

No pressure!

Warming up for XC I didn't feel too bad, looking back maybe I was a tad complacent but as with horses, you very quickly get reminded that you need to wake up and smell the roses.

He wouldn't go down to the start box, Carrot pretty much had to lead him. I nearly soiled myself right there.

But stop watch set off and we were away.

Not too bad a jump at the first, a wooden palisade shared with the 90. Down to another plain upright at two which he jumped ok too. I was very mindful of not going too fast, at this level we would be heavily penalised for our usual speed. Number 3 was the smallest log you've ever seen, he looked and nearly stopped so I really got after him! Dick! And that's where the wheels started to fall off.

He spooked at all the other jumps leading down to ours fences, some spooks were so exaggerated that I was left hanging half off. He got to fence 4 on the duffest stride because of looking at everything else and we nearly parted company. Fence 5 was a rail with a banner alongside and thank goodness I've had a banner up in the field at home because this was actually okay!

We had a massive spook on the way down to number 6; a roll top just before a mound with number 7; a skinny hanging log on top. I focused on the three strides up to 7 in my approach, thinking ahead and being a good and well prepared rider.

He put in the dirtiest stop ever at 6. The f*cking simple b*astard rolltop, it was sod all to look at. I tried to kick him over, desperate not to have a 20 to add. I kicked, growled, heaved, but it was over, it was all f*cking over.

20 penalties, I represented and of course he jumped it like it was nothing! I'm so f*cking disappointed. That was my win, I wanted it so much, I've never been bothered about a placing but today I felt utterly awful.

7 the hanging log jumped fine, he got a smack into 7b because I was gutted and because he was being a spooky little knob. In hindsight, I should have done that earlier because he jumped round the rest of the course like it was nothing! The bank at 10, hedge at 11, in the water and out of a skinny at 15/16... he answered every question right.

He spooked horribly at the last fence and I came through the finish with tears in my eyes. These were not tears of pride. They were tears of frustration, of disappointment, of all the hard f*cking work I've done to get his confidence up, all for nothing. I felt drained, I still do. My husband's face... he felt it too.

We walked back, washed him off and went to the scoreboard for a bit more torture. I'd have had a win; clear by nearly 10 points. I just wanted to go home.

Now in reflection, I feel stupid. I took my eye off the ball, I planned too far ahead, I didn't do all I could have done. It was MY fault. It was not bad luck, it was bad judgment and bad reactions.

This sport can be won or lost in a split second and for everything to come together on one day is a pure miracle but...

We are progressing, we are getting better, we are still learning and I'm not disappointed anymore. He isn't a push button pony and anyone else would struggle to get him round the dressage for a sub 40 let alone a sub 30 or in the start box!! He is sharp, tricky and you have to make him think it's all his idea... but that's what I love him so much.

He's not easy, but my word is he rewarding. We might have lost our first red one today, but it was never really ours to start with and I will never think that way again, you don't win just by getting the best marks. That might determine what colour piece of folded satin and cardboard you go home with but winning is empathy, understanding and education, and that's all that really matters.

Horses are not machines, yet we use them for our enjoyment, what right do I have to be angry when he doesn't act perfectly?

I also thought people would laugh at me for doing the 80 and not being up there in the placings too. But that's another thing I need to stop thinking about!

Lots of love as always

Vic and Pat xxxx

~

And there it was, my educational 2018. Ending the season as we started; still lacking in confidence and still only jumping 80cms. But look at the lessons we've learnt and how much different those things will make 2019 and the rest of our lives together. I am more determined than I have ever been in my whole life.

I have stopped worrying about what other people think of me. I have embraced the feeling of only having myself to disappoint and I will come out next year ready to succeed. I want to win far more than I did before, but not a red rosette. I want to win the trust of my beautiful horses, I want to win the admiration of my devoted husband and more than anything, I want to win a smile over every single finish line I cross.

**THE FINAL LESSON**: It is absolutely NOT about the placing, the fancy show jacket, the shininess of your lorry or the price you paid for your horse. It is about the empathy, love and understanding that you give to your animals, it's about what you take from each experience; good or bad. Don't think you can't turn a bad day on paper into the best day you've ever had, because I know you can. You get to decide how things turn out, you have that power. Why wouldn't you use it?

What are you waiting for? Make today amazing – you deserve it.